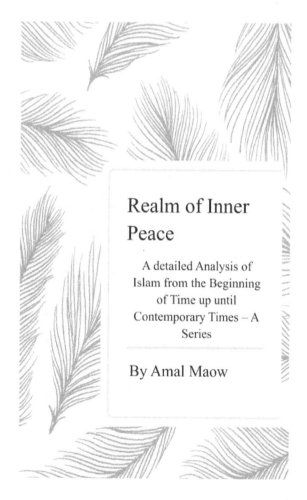

Realm of Inner Peace

A detailed Analysis of
Islam from the Beginning
of Time up until
Contemporary Times – A
Series

By Amal Maow

To access more books written by Amal Maow, visit:
www.amalmaow.com. This is a six-part series. The first book
of this series is called: Paradise State of Mind. The Realm of
Inner Peace, is a comprehensive review and a detailed
account of ancient and modern times, according to the
Qurān, that dissects the intricate complexities of all of the
stories contained therein.

Acknowledgements

I am in deep gratitude towards Allāh, the Creator of this universe for being my protector and friend. I would like to thank my loved ones, my family and friends – especially my mom Nadifa and my dad Abdullahi. I would not be where I am in life without their consistent support, love, and encouragement. Thank you for inspiring me to be the best version of myself every day. To the readers of this book, may you be elevated among the VIP in paradise, and find great benefit and insight from this book with every page you read. Thank you.

Realm of Inner Peace

Table of Contents

Part Two: Adam (A): The First Creations on Earth

In the Name of God, the Most Merciful, the Most Compassionate

AsalamuAlailkum – May God's Peace be Upon You

From the beginning of time, this was a greeting shared by the angels and the first man Adam (peace be upon him). It is also the greeting that over 1.6 billion Muslims in the world today greet each other with every day. To spread peace among one another, is something that was taught by all of the messengers of God, from Adam (peace be upon him), to Dawuud (peace be upon him), to Musa (peace be upon him), Isa/Jesus (peace be upon him), up until Prophet Muhammad (may God's peace be upon him and them all). It was the standard greeting that was exchanged by Adam (peace be upon him) and the angels of God. It was the brotherly greetings of peace that the prophet's uttered with their brethren and sisters in faith. To the reader of this book, I sincerely wish you peace and blessings. Why? This is because by reading this book, you are about to take part in a quest. A quest to understanding the true meaning of Islam. Islam through the mind, thoughts, and studies of a follower of Islam. Not through reports given to you –via- your television screen. Rather through credible verses of the Qur'an and authentic sayings of the Prophet Muhammad (peace be upon him).

It can be agreed that the Qur'an is a historical book, by the fact that it was revealed long ago. The Prophet Muhammad also lived almost 1,400 years ago. Therefore, in order to relate aspects of the Prophet's life and Qur'anic teachings to today's world; a thorough understanding and contextualization must take place. Together we will go back in time to the Genesis of the universe. Study the lifetime of the first man and series of Prophets all in historical order. Most of all there will be an extensive look into the Islamic view of Angels, the spiritual world, life and death. Each section narrating the stories of the Prophets will end with an analyzation of how it can be applied to today's world, and a look into detailed Qur'anic References concerning the Prophets and their lives. Towards the end hopefully, you will see the universe through an entirely different outlook.

The works contained in this book are inspired from the teachings of the Quran, narrations of Prophet Muhammad and important interpretations given by the early and classic commentators of Islam. Since, many past and contemporary books have been written from the lens of previous generations; this book was written so that the younger generation (my generation of Muslims) can relate. As time passes, we see new issues that arise, that have never been seen in earlier generations. As time passes, our world goes through many alterations big and small. The 20th century, has seen the advancement in technology and in the most accelerated pace that's ever been witnessed in human history. This book is to outline some of these changes we experience in our daily life, and weaving in the stories of the prophets so that it serves as a moral compass for you in these unique times.

This requires patience, from the part of the reader because this book involves a lot of prerequisite information before you get to the extraordinary aspects that will peak your interest. This book contains stories of the angels, the different categories of jinns, the human soul and what we know so far as well as information on the heavens and constellations. All of the research in this book is backed by extensive research (as well as memorization of the letters and meaning of all the verses in the Quran).

The Quran is a divine book revealed to the Prophet Muhammad through Angel Gabriel, from Allah (God). Revelations mentioned in the Quran by Allah include the Bible, Psalms of David, Scrolls of Abraham, Torah and Scriptures of Moses. Islam teaches that each of these contain divine words once revealed by God. Therefore, the books mentioned above contain some truth in it. God orders and commands the respect of each book He has revealed throughout the course of time.

The Quran, however is different. In the past prophets and messengers each received miracles that were quick glimpses of extraordinary actions that were outside of the scope of human abilities. For example,

Prophet Isa (Jesus), was known to cure the sick, in one case he cured a man with leprosy. In another case, he raised a man from the dead and brought him back to life. Prophet Moses, had the ability to do extraordinary things with his staff. He parted the sea, so that the Children of Israel can cross to the other side and escape the Pharaoh and his army. He also had the ability to radiate light from his hands, just by touching his chest. Prophet David had the ability to mold, carve, and bend iron and the toughest precious metals with his bare hands. He was a builder and a shepherd like many of the Prophets of God. Prophet and King Solomon, who was the son of King and Prophet David – also had the ability to control the winds, bring objects to him from far distances by the speed of light, connect with the spirit world, and understand the language of all animals in the world. These are some of the stories that God revealed in the Quran.

The Quran is different because it is not a miracle that lasts for a moment, a few minutes, or seconds. It is the only miracle that outlived all the messengers of Allah, and will remain so until the end times. Since the last messenger was Prophet Muhammad, Allah chose for the final message to be in the form of a book. That way, the message contained within this book will be a lasting miracle for all people, of all nations, until the end of the world.

The Quran is the last revelation to humankind. Allah has promised to protect it from all corruption, and changes. Almighty God, has made a promise when He said the following:

"And We have made the Qurān, easy to remember." Quran

The Quran is easy to remember, because it is very easy to memorize. In fact, children as old as the age of five memorize all 6,000 verses and 10,000+ pages of the Quran every day. Throughout the centuries, revelations sent by God to humankind like the Bible, the Torah, and the Psalms, were all changed or lost. Sometimes scriptures dating 3000 to 2000+ years old were lost and the message not fully intact, it happens. However, the Quran is the only book in the world that does not have missing parts, its story consistent, and its message complete and intact.

In fact, there are many parts that today's Bible that is missing. There are excavations that were made of the Book of Barnabus, which is said to be a part of the Bible that has been missing for years, written by one of the apostles who people claim knew Jesus (peace be upon him). Scholars of all faiths have agreed that the Book of Barnabus, which is known to be a part of the Bible matches the narration of Jesus (Isa) peace be upon him, contained within the Quran.

One example of some of the lines contained in the Book of Barnabus includes:

Jesus, weeping, said: "O Barnabas, it is necessary that I should reveal to you great secrets, which, after that I shall be departed from the world, you shall reveal to it." Then answered he that writes, weeping, and said: "Suffer me to weep, O master, and other men also, for that we are sinners. And you, that are a holy one and prophet of God, it is not fitting for you to weep so much."

Jesus answered: "Believe me, Barnabas that I cannot weep as much as I ought. For if men had not called me God, I should have seen God here as he will be seen in paradise, and should have been safe not to fear the day of judgment. But God knows that I am innocent, because never have I harbored thought to be held more than a poor slave. No, I tell you that if I had not been called God I should have been carried into paradise when I shall depart from the world, whereas now I shall not go thither until the judgment. Now you see if I have cause to weep."

"Know, O Barnabas, that for this I must have great persecution, and shall be sold by one of my disciples for thirty pieces of money. Whereupon I am sure that he who shall sell me shall be slain in my name, for that God shall take me up from the earth, and shall change the appearance of the traitor so that everyone shall believe him to be me; nevertheless, when he dies an evil death, I shall abide in that dishonor for a long time in the world. But when Muhammad shall come, the sacred Messenger of God, that infamy shall be taken away. And this shall God do because I have confessed the truth of the Messiah who shall give me this reward, that I shall be known to be alive and to be a stranger to that death of infamy.\\It is interesting to see that there are many inconsistencies within previous scriptures, and this has a lot to do with human tampering and changes which we will cover, with evidence and proof in the next chapters. This is the major reason why the Quran is a miracle. It is because since 1400+ years it has not been changed, the stories and theme within the Quran remain consistent, and its guidance firm and straight in all aspects for many nations in the world today.

What is the wisdom behind the Quran being easy to memorize?

It is so that it can be protected by those whom it is being protected from; in other words, humans. God places his words in the hearts of those that he loves, and they carry these words with them for the rest of their lives. This means, if the Quran is every changed slightly, or a new edition of the Quran is put in place, or even if all scriptures were to be thrown out into the ocean; the Quran will be the only one that can be replicated back to how it was in a matter of days. That is because millions of Muslims around the world have memorized it by heart. This way of preserving the Quran is, in itself, a miracle from God Almighty.

The first man and prophet in Islam is known to be Adam (peace be upon him). Many of the Prophets mentioned in the Quran are also mentioned in the Bible and the Torah. Since Islam, Christianity, and Judaism are all a part of the Abrahamic teachings; there are some similarities. Nonetheless, there are also major differences in each teaching that sets them apart. In this work, the main differences and similarities will be laid through a close look at the historic evidences. Lastly, information pertaining to the religious historical landmarks, important regions, and ancient discoveries will all be covered in light of the Quran revelations in the next series. It is only after developing a deeper understanding of the initial history, that one can make sense of today's world. Therefore, it will be during the remainder of this journey will culminate with a closer look into contemporary times.

The most important aspect of these series are the lifetimes of the Prophets, which will be discussed in detail in the next book. This book will be focusing the beginning of times. If you are accustomed to the Prophets mentioned in the Bible; then you wouldn't have a hard time remembering the Prophet's mentioned in the Quran. In chronological order the Prophets mentioned in the Quran are the following: Adam, Enoch (Idris), Noah, Hud, Saleh, Abraham, Ishmaeel, Isaac, Jacob, Lot,

Joseph, Job, Shu'ayb, Aaron, Moses, Samuel, David, Solomon, Elijah, Dhul-Khilf, Jonha, Zechariah, John, and Jesus (May Gods peace and blessings be upon them all.)

Imagine the greatest gatherings that people think would be amazing to be a part of. This could be any gathering in the world; the Emmy's, the Grammies, the Golden Globe Awards, Noble Peace Prize events; whichever they may be. The names I mentioned above are more important and weigh more than the name of any celebrity you can think of in the world today. There is only one reason why. These are names that were mentioned by God in all previous scriptures, and in the final scripture, the Quran.

These are humans who have reached the peak of hardship, and struggle; and never lost faith in God, through it all. These are humans who had the greatest failures in life, but still, they never wavered in their connection with the One who is Greater than this whole universe; Allah. These are humans who have experienced, sadness, heartbreak, difficulties that they thought they would never get out of; and submitted themselves to God in every single situation. How did they do that? By internalizing that nothing in this world could be possessed or owned, not even happiness; we only experience, and the only One true thing that matters is acquainting our soul with the one who Created it.

This was their mindset throughout every difficulty. When they lost someone, the prophets of God knew, that people could not be possessed, they could only be experienced for a short time. They knew that material things could not be possessed, that we will one day leave it all behind. They reminded themselves of the day that their bodies would no longer belong to them, when it would become a part of the earth, which also belongs to Allah. This is why their names and stories are mentioned in the Quran (the final revelation) so that their stories could serve as a moral compass, and guidance to all humans on earth. There is a saying, "only a fool learns from his own mistakes, a wise person learns from the mistakes of others." The Quran serves as a collection of stories that are meant to guide a person away from potential risks in life to their physical, mental, emotional, and spiritual well-being. It is by equipping humanity with knowledge and wisdom, that guidance will soon follow. This book will serve as a scope to understand that wisdom and guidance contained within the Quran.

Since the past is vastly different from contemporary times, this book will give present examples, along with contemporary commentaries to give life to the marvelous stories of the Prophets. Often in today's society history is not given the brilliance it truly deserves. With this narrative of reality, adventure, action and suspense the reader will find themselves in another realm. The realm of the past and its many mysteries.

Let it be known that there was extensive effort to use credible evidences regarding each component presented in this work. Upon the completion of the book, it shall be apparent to the reader that the message of every Prophet is one. Each prophet strived for one particular goal. To deliver the message to their people by the command of their Lord. To encourage the worship of God, alone and to achieved utmost harmony with His divine teachings by incorporating the true message into daily activities.

The message of each prophet came with three factors; a miracle, good news, and a warning. The miracle was generally given to each prophet to show their people that they are indeed men who were chosen and sent by God. The good news came after the miracle. The good news was that there is a God who created humans and if they obeyed his message and lived righteously they will earn heaven. The warning was if they saw the truth and decided to disobey a punishment will be sent upon them.

With the lifetime of the various prophets these factors will be analyzed deeply by taking a close look into the time and the circumstances. Each prophetic message and miracle confirmed the existence of God, that all aspects of life are under His divine control and all of creation submits to His will. Moreover, it is because of this that there is none worthy of worship but Him. God is Ever-Existent, and Ever-Lasting, and every aspect of life is under His knowledge. When each message was sent upon mankind through the many Prophets, it was emphasized that each individual is responsible for his own actions, and that no individual bears the burden of another. Lastly, each prophet warned of a day when mankind will return to their Lord and Judgement will take place at an appointed time.

What about the name "Islam"? Where did this name come from, what was belief of God called before, and what were believers in God called before Islam? It must be understood first that Islam is a divine teaching and a way of lide. Its meaning is derived from the root word in Arabic "salm" which means "peace". The entire meaning of Islam is peaceful submission of the will of God. What is the Will of God? The Will of God, is a divine attribute of God. The attribute encompasses everything that is happening now, and will happen in the future is known to God already. That, every factor that happens in life happens because he ordained it and allowed it to happen. It is through the acceptance of the Will of God that a human being can attain full peace and serenity in their lives. The very air that we breathe every second of our lives shows that we are submitting to the Will of God. This is because God in his ultimate Knowledge and Wisdom ordained for us to live before the creation of the universe. Thus, just by living and breathing we are forming an acceptance with his Divine Order that He has preordained for us as humans.

Hence, the entire meaning of Islam; "peaceful submission to the Will of God", covers all of mankind in general, both Muslims and non-Muslims alike. Whether a person is a Muslim or not the moment they are born and take their first breath they are willingly accepting what was prescribed to them beforehand; and that is to live. The meaning of Islam alone shows that Islam is not a teaching for only one group of people, rather it is for all of mankind.

Many people question what the Will is. It all began before the creation of the universe, in which God in his ultimate Wisdom recorded all that will happen in a 'prescribed scroll' called 'lawhil-mahfudh'. This scroll contains everything that was, is, and will be. Every detail in the universe and what is beyond human scope and knowledge was determined by Almighty God. Now, this does not mean that everyone is forced to do what has been determined. It just clarifies that God is the All-Knowing and the All-Wise. Regardless of what was determined to happen. God in His divine nature has knowledge of all past and future occurrences. It is because we don't know what will happen in the future, and are not burdened with knowledge of our destiny; that we have a chance to make our own decision comfortably as human beings. This system of living that God has adjusted for humans through his ultimate mercy gives us the chance to conduct our lives according to our needs without worry.

As humans, we are given the choice by being presented with multiple decisions in our daily lives. These small decisions that we make in life are what leads us to the ultimate outcome of our future. Although this future of ours is in Gods ultimate knowledge, the outcome of our lives, and the path we choose to take is entirely under our own risk and completely our choice. Incidentally, my choice to write this book was in Gods knowledge aforetime. However, I was given the choice to abandon this intention or carry it on. Moreover, I was given a privilege. A privilege that is bestowed upon all human beings, to think, reflect, and ponder before making final decisions. It all began with my reflection on the state of Muslims today, and a choice to make a difference. I thank Almighty God for giving me the resolve and the heart to write. In all sincerity, I am forever grateful that Almighty God has given me the chance to breathe another day.

That being said, Islam is the final name God has chosen for his Divine teachings.

"On this day, we have completed your religion for you and bestowed upon you Our blessings, and have ordained for you Islam as the teaching of God." –Surah Maedah (Chapter: The Table Spread)

Consequently, the nations who received scriptures revealed to them from God, had their own names in their own scripture. As God states in the Quran, the Christians are called, '*Nasaara*' or The Helpers and the Jews are called "*Yahuud*" or named after the first son of Jacob (peace be upon him) *Yahuda*. Even though they were called by different naes at the time their specific scripture was sent, since they all worshipped only One God they can all be considered Muslims. Since the meaning of "Muslim" is 'one who peacefully submits to the Will of God'. Consequently, the Prophets from the time of Adam to the last Prophet; were all Muslims. A Muslim finds within himself peace and serenity with other fellow humans by following the moral and noble ethical guidelines conveyed to them by the Prophets.

As a disclaimer, some believe that Islam was "born" at a certain time period in Saudi Arabia. This could have never been far from the truth. "Islam" was a name given to humankind by the Creator of the universe during the lifetime of Prophet Mohamed. However, the concept of Islam was present from the first Prophet until the last Prophet. And each one of these Prophets taught us that God is one and that he should be worshipped alone. The revelations sent aforetime may have not been called Islam but they all promoted the same underlying principle. That the purpose of our life is one, and we are all human beings under the same Creator. To respect the one who gave us life enough to give Him credit and worship Him as he deserves. With that being explained, the representation I took regarding the stories of the Prophets is solely from the translation and commentary of *Sahih International Translation*; while narrating the lifetime of the Prophets the interconnecting and related verses will be states. Through this method the actual accuracy of God Almighty's statements will not be countered. In addition, the reader will have proof the Divine revelations of God when it comes to the account of each Prophet. Other Qur'anic translations aside from Sahih International Translation will include; Pickthall, AbdalHaqq, Hilal/Khan, Yusuf Ali, Maudud, Arberry, Aisha, and Asad. There will be references towards the completion of each section on the verse, and the commentary and the translation used. In addition, each Qur'anic verse will be printed in bold and quoted to differentiate between the verse and the rest of the passage.

There will be footnotes to conclude with the different passage and text for utmost detail. The explanation of these footnotes will be found toward the end of each page. At the end of the book thorough definitions of certain Islamic terminology will be given; specifically, in the glossary of terms.

Additionally, thought provoking questions, and sentiments will be posed to keep the ball rolling. Through this, further analyzation of interesting topics and conclusions may be reached. Nonetheless, the conclusion will be based upon reality and its foundation will be Islam. The underlying effort in this work has been to stick to credible sources, and precise and clear interpretations. All questionable materials have been steered away from this book. That way the ultimate goal of this writing will be built upon solid foundation and credible material. Furthermore, even after the effort to present sound material mistake may be found, as I am human. In the process, if there are any mistakes, it was due to my own limitation. Therefore, I ask the reader of the book to forgive my short comings. Above all, I seek the ultimate forgiveness of mu Creator, since all Glory and Greatness belongs to Him. With humility, sincerity, and without further a due I present to you Through a Muslims Eyes. I hope readers from all nations, backgrounds, and beliefs accept this humble effort. In the end all Glory, Praise, and Exaltation is to the Mighty Creator of the Universe. All peace and blessings to each and every noble Prophet, and most of all to the reader of this book; may the most Merciful bless you with guidance now and forever.

Part 1: The Genesis of the Universe

"Blessed is He who made constellation in the sky and placed there in a brilliant lamp, and a moon giving light!" Qur'an 25:61

In the beginning, way before the creation of the universe there was God. He is the Ever Existent who had no beginning and the Everlasting who has no end. You may have asked yourself once, "then who created God?" God was not created by anyone. He just is and still is. He is not in need of space nor time. Rather space and time are both aspects that need Him. Although His Divine being is not enough for the human mind to grasp, out of His ultimate mercy He revealed His message to humankind various times. In those revelations God described Himself in an estimated capacity fit for the human intellect. The intriguing yet merciful element of conveying His presence was by informing the populace through their own language; so that they may understand the purpose of existence on earth.

He will continue to be the first and will go on being the Everlasting. Time is not of essence to His divine being. Rather, time is a man-made concept used for the purpose of measurement regarding the cycle of night and day in the celestial orbit of the universe. In fact, God is not in need of time, while the creations that bring the alterations of night and day (the sun and the moon) are in need of Him. The creation of the heavens and the earth were brought into existence due to His Power and Knowledgeable presence. Without Him, there would have been nothing. Through Him, there came the existence of something. That 'something' is the universe.

Looking around, we are entrapped in mass quantities of space. The amount of space this entire universe takes up is classified as matter and all around us there are complex particles that make up the composition of this enormous universe. Elements ranging from hydrogen, to oxygen, and nitrogen among many others. All of these complex systems to the tiniest speck of atom contained in each one of them have an origin. This origin must have come from some intelligence that has the capability to activate the properties in which these elements are formed. Power. All of this is from Power, and that Power is God Almighty Himself.

The beginnings of the universe are illustrated in many different beliefs and cultures. People of all origins even have their own assumptions and opinions that may revolve around their own sets of belief and cultures. Many assumptions are similar to one another, while others are very different and unique. Nonetheless there are three books in this world that agree on the creation of the universe; that the universe was created in six days, the Torah, the Gospel, and the Qur'an.

What do all three Abrahamic faiths have to say about the genesis of the universe? Since thr Torah and the Gospel are mentioned in the Qur'an let us see what is written in the main scriptures when it comes to the Genesis of the universe.

The Torah and the Gospel (Old and New Testament) states: "And God saw all that He had made, and found it very good. And there was evening and there was morning, the sixth day. The heaven and the earth were finished, and all their array." Genesis 1:31 – 2:1

The Quran states: "Indeed, your Lord is Allah, who created the heavens and the earth in six days" Quran 7:54

This is clearly what the scriptures say, how come all three came into full agreement with one another? It seems this must not be a coincidence. This is because god Almighty specifically stated in the Qur'an that the Torah and the Gospel were once books sent by God through the Angel Gabriel and finally to the given Prophets. The Torah and Gospel were sent for the same purpose that the Qur'an was sent for; to reveal to mankind the truth of this universe and what is to come after.

The universe is vast, in it are many galaxies and worlds unknown to humankind. Thus, the reason why the beginning chapters of the Qur'an begin with the following:

"In the Name of God the most Merciful, the most Gracious, All Praise is due to the Lord of the Worlds."

Notice how God Almighty did not say the Lord of the World. Rather, the word 'world' was made plural. This means that there are domains unknown to mankind and are only in the knowledge of the most Wise the All-encompassing. This verse itself shows how limited we are as human beings. That only God is the Knower of all things since He created it to begin with.

What are these 'worlds'? Well, since there are countless galaxies those we known of and some we don't it can be a physical world unknown to humankind. On the other hand, it can also mean the spiritual worlds that are beyond the human senses.

Nonetheless, the world we are most familiar with is ours. So, what does God have to say about this world? In the Qur'an, this world is called 'dunya' most closely related to the word 'life' or 'earth' in the English vocabulary. All together the word 'dunya' means: 'the life of this world'.

The creator of the heavens, and the Earth is God. As stated in the following verses of the Qur'an:

"Or, who originated Creation, then repeats it, and who gives you sustenance from heaven and earth? Can there be another God besides Allah? Say, "Bring forth your argument, if you are telling the truth." Quran 27:64

The above verse specifically begins with the cause of the universe. Stating that the originator of all of creation is none other than God Himself. Notice that this verse is a direct commandment that is challenging anyone who has proof against the existence of God. During the time of the Prophet Muhammad (peace be upon him) the pagan's believed that there was a God, however they used stone idols that they molded with their own hands as manifestations of God. They also used stone idols as intermediaries between them and God. These stone idols were elements of worship that they used to get closer to the Creator. They knew that this universe was created by the most Powerful, the Sovereign, and the Almighty. Regardless of this belief, most chose to ignore the signs that the verses of the Qur'an showed from time to time. Thus, the reason why God Almighty challenged; "…Bring forth your argument, if you are telling the truth." This is because they couldn't argue with that core principle due to the fact they themselves believed in the Supreme Being. It is because of their desire to continue worshipping the idols that they refused to acknowledge the revelation.

God Almighty stressed in many verses that He is the Originator of the heavens, the earth and all that is in between.

"See they not how Allah originates creation, then repeats it: truly that is easy for Allah. Say: "Travel through the earth and see how Allah originated creation,' so will Allah produce a later creation: For Allah has power over all things." Quran 17:99

As stated in a commentary of the Holy Qur'an regarding this verse: "The originating of creation is the creation of primeval matter. The repetition of the process of creation goes on constantly, for at every moment new, processes are being called into being by the creative power of Allah, and according to His laws. And the final creation as far as man is concerned will be in the Ma'ad (later life), when the whole world as man sees it will be entirely newly created on a different plane. As far as Allah is concerned, there is nothing final, no first and last, for He is infinite. He was before our First and will be after our last."

Regarding the verse that stats, travel through the earth we see this is repeated many times in the Qur'an. It is to show that as humans we should see beyond our own scope. To witness the regal creations of the

Almighty Lord we must first travel beyond our own element. The commentary of this verse in the Holy Qur'an goes on to say; "we shall see the wonderful things in His Creation, the Grand Canyon and the Niagara in Canada, beautiful harbors like that at Sydney Australia, mountains like Fujiyama, the Himalayas, and Elburz in Asia, the Nile with its wonderful cataracts in Africa, the Fiords of Norway, the Geysers of Iceland, the city of the midnight sun in Tromsoe, and innumerable wonders everywhere. But wonders upon wonders disclosed in the constitution of matter itself, the atom, and the forces of energy, as also is the instincts of animals, and the minds and capacities of man. And there is no limit to these things. Worlds upon worlds are created and transformed every moment, within and presumably beyond man's vision. From what we know we can judge of the unknown."

Seeing all of this and knowing in our heart that it was created in just six earth days creates within a person a humbling sense of feeling. That, all of these sights are often taken for granted. This wasn't on accident, it's our homeland. Although we are mere mortals compared to God, He has still furnished our surroundings as a source of beauty and a sign for those who choose to reflect.

God Almighty reiterates in the Qur'an once again:

"Your Guardian Lord is Allah, who created the heavens and the earth in six days, then he settled Himself on the Throne: He draws night as a veil over day, each seeking the other in rapid succession: And the sun, the moon, and the stars, all are subservient under his command. Verily, His are the creation and the command. Blessed be Allah, the Cherisher and Sustainer of the worlds!"

Once again, the above verses dictate that the origins of the universe were all under the control of the Creator. All of the most influential celestial objects: the sun, moon, and the stars are running in orbit by His command. Without his order, command, supervision, power, and guidance these objects will all seize to function. The initiating stages of the universe have been studied by archeologists and geologists alike. Most of the main claims are very similar to what God Almighty states in the Qur'an, concepts such as the Big Bang, the expansion of the universe, the shape of the earth, and the function of the orbits which will be discussed in the later chapters in this book.

A day in the sight of God Almighty can be compared to 1,000 years. Thus, the six days in which the universe was created – is equal to a thousand years in the sight of God. However, God, in his divine presence experienced those days like it was just six. While on the other hand human beings would look at thousands of years as a very long time. This just shows how intellectually limited we are in every capacity, when it comes to time itself. It also shows that God Almighty is Al-Sabuur the patient, He is perfect in all aspects.

In the Divine Speech of God Himself, He states the following:

"Allah! There is no God but He, the Living, the Self-Subsisting, the supporter of all. No slumber can seize Him nor sleep. His are all things in the heavens and on earth. Who is thee that can intercede in His presence except as He permits? He knows what appears to His creatures before or after or behind them. Nor shall they compass anything of His knowledge except as He wills. His throne extends over the heavens and the earth, and He feels no fatigue in guarding and preserving them, for He is the Highest. The Supreme in Glory." Surah Al-Baqara | Ayat Al-Kursi (The verse of the throne).

The above verse is the only verse in the Qur'an speaks of God Almighty in detail. What's better than knowing who the Most Supreme is, the One who is responsible for the entire Creation of the universe? As you already read, God Almighty does not sleep nor rest. He is the sole caregiver of all that is contained within the universe. Some may believe that God rested on the last day of the creation of the universe; but that cannot be true. The reason is due to the fact that if God were even to rest for a split second this entire universe would be thrown odd course. Sleeping is a state in which a being is unaware and God is

All-Aware. There comes the main point that we must understand. God Almighty in His Divine characteristics is not in need of sleep, while human beings need rest. Just like God does not need time or space, He is not in need of sleep either. Sleep is a phenomenon gifted to us by God Almighty. Saying that 'God rested' is limiting God and/or comparing Him to having human characteristics. The Creator of this universe must be One who is greater than this universe; and all of its influences.

The genesis of the Universe is the sole beginning of all that there is now, and all that there was before. It was when God Almighty initiated the beginnings of creation. What exactly was there before the creation of the universe? Only God knows the detailed analysis to that question. However, some things are presented to us in the Quran which will be discussed in detail throughout the book.

Introduction

He is the First, He is the Last, He is the Eternal, the

Ever Existent, the Ever Lasting He is Allah

The genesis of the universe is the sole beginning of all that there is now, and all that there was before. It was when God Almighty initiated the beginning of creation. What exactly was there before the creation of this great universe? Only God knows the detailed analysis to that question, this will be thoroughly investigated through evidence from the Quranic texts and Hadith (the Hadith are a collection of sayings from the Prophet Muhammad, which have been collected by his most trusted companions and passed down orally from generation to generation.). For those of you who do not believe in God, the answer to this will also forever remain a mystery.

However, an abundant number of scenes detailing this occasion is depicted to mankind in the Qur'an -- the last revelation to mankind. Before taking a look into these descriptions we must understand that Allah is independent of time. Therefore, concerning His Divine reality there is no before or after. According to the Quran Allah (swt) reveals that He is the only Creator. Allah, many times reiterates that He is the only Sustainer over the entire universe. His existence is not shaped by time or space, for that matter. Therefore, the Most High has no beginning nor an end. Out of the number of names that Allah exalts Himself with in the Quran, three of them are Al- Awal, Al-Akhir and Al-Samad; which mean -- the first, the last, and the eternal.

In terms of mans conscious intellect, time only exists when something exists. So as long as we exist, we will be completely wrapped within in the phenomenon of time. Thus, since time is the essence of our original nature it is much easier for us to try to comprehend and relate the existence of Allah with this limited measurement. We must know, the existence of the Creator of this universe can not be measured. What Allah explains to us in His final revelation, is that time has a beginning and an end. However, He who is the Creator of time does not have a beginning or an end. He tells us that man who was created along with time has a beginning and an end, but He Exalted above man is Ever Existent and Ever Lasting.

For example, mankind in our limited sense of the Divine Reality might say, "there was a time when the universe didn't exist." In reality, what we should say is, "the universe didn't exist." because the creation of time and the universe both come in the same package; they are both the artistic forms of Allahs magnificent creativity that we will never be able to fully understand. Thus, we know that if the universe does not exist then time does not exist and vice versa. So, the question is what was there before the subjectively perplexing aspect of time came into being? What we don't know for sure is if there was another universe like this one or perhaps a different realm. What we do know is that there was God. He was the first. So, what exactly does Allah say about Himself?

In the following verses Allah (swt) reveals to all of mankind, the reality of His existence before He initiated the creation of time and the creation of this great universe. The most Merciful explains this relative to the realm of time -- in order that mankind might understand. The usage of His exalted names, "The First" and "The Last" are repeated to explain to us that; compared to His Creation He is "The First" but in general we must know that He is Ever-Existent, compared to His creation He is "The Last" but in general we must know that He is Ever-Lasting. Thus, the concept of time is only intertwined with the concept of Allah's reality just for us to grasp and understand His nature relative to ours. That He is indeed Exalted above His creation.

"Say, "He is Allah, [who is] One, Allah the Eternal refuge." 112:1-2

"He is the First and the Last, the Outermost and the Innermost and He has full knowledge of all things," - The Qur'an, 57:3

"Allah - (there is) no God except Him, the Ever-Living the Sustainer of all that exists." The Quran 3:2 and 2:255

38

"And everlasting will be the Face of your Lord, Owner of Majesty and Honor. (Surat Ar-Rahman 55:27)

When a man wants to send a letter to another individual. They must start with introducing themselves in a way that the one receiving his message can grasp who he is as a person. Therefore, the one revealing aspects about himself in the letter will explain accordingly, so that the receiver can understand. Otherwise the letter will be of no use and its message will not be able to properly get across. The same way in the Quran Allah Almighty, explains His characteristics in detail. This is so that we may understand, and get to know who our Creator is on a deeper level. So that we may know and understand what is it that Allah the Highest is pleased with, and is it that causes His Divine anger.

"and We have revealed the Book to you explaining clearly everything"
(16:89)
"And We sent down the book to you for the express purpose that you should make clear to them those things in which they differ, and so that it should be a guide and mercy to those who believe". (16:64).

So, what does this tell us? Allah explaining to us that He is the First and the Last, is relative to our existence. He is First compared to us. He is the last compared to us. However, He is also "Al-Samad" the ever-lasting. It gives a brief explanation of what we need to know about

Allah's Divine Reality. By 'need', I mean what applies to us as human beings and what knowledge from the Almighty will benefit us for our temporary stay in this world. For example, asking questions such as "What was there before Allah?" we will never know, and it was never described to us in the Quran. What was explained to us in the Quran was the initiation of Creation; which is in fact knowledge pertaining to our origins and where we come from. This knowledge of our origin and the origin of the universe is of benefit to us. It is because upon knowing this reality we will be able to witness the Power of Allah and appreciate His Might and Wisdom. All aspects regarding our Creator and His reality beyond the creation of time and man is not necessary for us to know because that is pertaining to His Divine Being only. Anything pertaining to the realm of time and the creation of this universe has been explained in the Quran in detail (which will be covered later on). Of course, what God explained to us in the Quran is only a fraction of His infinite knowledge. It is because of this that what we know is very little, and more importantly what we don't know is even greater.

Before understanding the Creation of the universe, we must first familiarize ourself with its Creator. He has explained a numerous amount of his Exalted attributes in many parts of the Quran. One may ask, "so what is the wisdom behind these attributes of God?" Each and every one of these attributes are a sole part in Allah being the Only True Creator and the only Deserving Creator of the worlds. As explained earlier, in order for a recipient of the letter to understand who its deliverer is; it must be explained within the letter. The message of the Quran is authored by the One and Only Creator. A significant feature of the Quran is that its verses often end with a pair of Allahs attributes, names that describe His ultimate Sovereignty and Glory. Thus, the entire Quran is scattered with references of Allahs personality. There will not be a page that one comes across without being overcome with a Divine characteristic of God. This is so that the reader of the Quran knows who their Creator, Sustainer and Fashioner is. So that, through our own limited characteristics we are able to grasp the Greatness of our Lord. The genesis of the universe begins with Allah, so we must ask ourselves first; who is Allah?

"He is Allah, the One besides whom there is no other deity, Knower of the unseen and the Witnessed. He is the most Merciful, the Compassionate. He is Allah, the One besides whom there is no other deity, the Sovereign, the Holy One, the Source of Peace, the Bestower of Safety, the Guardian, the Exalted, the Irresistible, the Supreme. Glory be to Allah above whatever they associate with Him! He is Allah, the Creator, the Maker, the Fashioner. To Him belong the beautiful Names. Whatever is in the heavens and whatever is on the earth glorifies Him, and He is the exalted, the Wise." Qur'an [59:22-24]

The above verses stated by God Himself, is an explanation of the Divine nature of Allah the Highest. These verses are in Surah Al-Hashr; a chapter in the book of Allah called *The Gathering*.

Who is Allah (swt)? Allah is the name of God. This name does not belong to any group, and it is not specified into any category. The name of Allah is simply universal. It is the name that God has chosen for Himself. This is the name that has been uttered by the first man to walk this earth, the angels, prophets, messengers, and those who believed in the message and followed them. Each nation expressed the name of God according to the language God sent His revelation in. For example; in Aramaic (the language of Jesus of Nazareth) the name for God was *Alaha*, in Hebrew (the language of David and Moses) the name for God was *Elohim*, and in Arabic (the language of Muhammad) the name for God was revealed as *Allah*. The similarity of Alaha, Allah, and Elohim lies in the fact that Hebrew, Arabic, and Armaic are closely related languages.

Until today people of many backgrounds, and languages who have accepted Gods way all across the world and developed this beautiful name into their language when speaking about God Almighty. Indeed, it is important to note that both Arab speaking Christians, Jews and Arab speaking Muslims refer to God as 'Allah' also. Allah is the most Powerful, and he is infinitely most exalted than his creation.

The Highest is nothing like what He created, and remains unique to all that surrounds Him. The nature of the Almighty is so great and vast that it does not compare to any. The attributes of the Almighty are entirely ever existent, while the attributes of mankind are finite and are influenced by emotions, intellectual limitations, characteristic deviancy, and the social environment. Humankind are selfish, while Allah the Highest is Selfless. The Exalted Creator of this universe is not in need of His creation, rather the creation is in need of Him. God Almighty is dis-attached from emotions and is above all its influence. It must be understood that just because Allah (the Highest) is the most Merciful, it does not mean He will have Mercy on those who transgress against His commands. The most High is a morally upright God, who is Just and Fair when given the circumstances and Loving and Merciful when given the circumstances.

Allah is the Creator of heaven and its bliss, and He is also the Creator of Hell and its punishment. Since both of these realities were created by Allah the Highest, it will serve as the abode of whom it has been prescribed. Heaven is beyond our imagination and is beautiful in every way, therefore those who are deserving of its bliss will enter. Hell is the place in which the soul will be farthest from the grace of his Lord, condemned, and punished; therefore, those who are deserving of its punishment will enter. Although Allah is eternally Merciful and Loving, His eternal Mercy will be enveloped around those who deserve the eternal Mercy and Love of their Creator. Consequently, since Allah is Fair and Just, His Judgment will be either a swift brief punishment or a graceful eternity to those who will be deserving of either. In the final revelation to mankind the most High describes Himself with many characteristics or attributes. These attributes are eternal, and often simultaneous through his ultimate Power and Will.

The attributes of Allah (the most High) are his characteristics and the very nature of His being. Every single creation in this universe exhibit their own way of personality and characteristic traits that are unique from one another. Some people are more patient than others in extreme circumstances, while others break down in the face of adversity the moment it touches them. There are people are very enduring and forbearing in the most burdensome of situations, while others give up mentally and spiritually the moment a dreadful situation arises in their lives. Each and every creation of God are similar yet different in so many ways. And so these very characteristic traits that man was created with is to show that a limited human can exhibit all of these qualities, therefore the Creator of all that exists must be One who has the ability to personify His own Divine attributes in any way He (the most High) wishes. These attributes were expressed in the Quran (the final message) in so many ways. This is in order that mankind understand their Originator and Maker, and have a firm idea of who their Creator is.

The way in which the Creator (most High Allah) expresses His Divine attributes make sense. In order for a recipient of a message to understand where a letter came from they must be able to know who it is from. The Mercy of the Creator is such that, not only has He explained the final message is from Him but He also adds a detailed account of what we should know about His Divine Reality. And the Creator of the Children of Adam does this in a way where many verses end with two names that describe Him. Often verses in the Qur'an end with "...and He is the most compassionate, the most merciful", "...and He is the most knowing, the Wisest", "...and He is the most High, the most Great", "...and He is the All-Hearing, the All-Seeing".

The Divine Names

God took for himself the name" Allah". The name Allah is neither masculine nor feminine. Rather, He is incomparable to any living creature He created. While most Christians I know may argue "God created us in his image." Muslims believe God is nothing like his creation. He is unable to be perceived by any of the senses, since we have no knowledge of the unseen. Among the names He chose for himself includes, the most powerful and the all-knowing; the giver and the taker; the wise and the generous; while He is the most merciful to his creation, He can also be stern in punishment if needed. His attributes and names that are used to praise Him are 99.

To name a few; the Almighty, the Majestic, the Creator, the Forgiver, the Honorable and the Guardian of his creation. Allah describes himself in the Quran in many ways. The most notable aspect of Allah's attributes are the 99 names of Allah, which are mentioned in the Quran and by Prophet Mohamed (May the Mercy and Peace of Allah be upon Him). These names now known to mankind are the names God used in the Quran to describe Himself. Below is a list of the names of God found in the Quran, it must be noted that there are many names that we do not know about that only the angels, and a few select people on earth use or know about (often through inspiration or unknowingly calling Allah one of His other names) nonetheless below are the main names we know of that are great to use during prayer

| 1 | Ar Rahman | الرحمن | The most Beneficent |

2	Ar Raheem	الرحيم	The Most Merciful
3	Al Malik	الملك	The King
4	Al Quddus	القدوس	The Most Holy
5	As Salam	السلام	The Ultimate Provider of Peace
6	Al Mu'min	المؤمن	The Guardian of Faith
7	Al Muhaymin	المهيمن	The Protector
8	Al Aziz	العزيز	The Mighty
9	Al Jabbaar	الجبار	The Compeller
10	Al Mutakabbir	الْمُتَكَبِّرُ	The Dominant One
11	Al Khaaliq	الخالق	The Creator
12	Al Baari	البارئ	The Evolver

13	Al Musawwir	المصور	Flawless Shaper
14	Al Ghaffaar	الغفار	The Ever-Forgiving
15	Al Qahhaar	القهار	The All Subduer
16	Al Wahhaab	الوهاب	The Bestower
17	Ar Razzaaq	الرزاق	The Ever-Providing; The Sustainer
18	Al Fattaah	الفتاح	The Ultimate Judge; The Opener of All Portals; The Victory Giver
19	Al Alim	العليم	The All-Knowing; The Omniscient
20	Al Qaabidh	القابض	The Restrainer; The Straightener
21	Al Baasit	الباسط	The Expander; The Munificent
22	Al Khaafidh	الخافض	The Abaser
23	Ar Raafi'	الرافع	The Exalter

24	Al Mu'izz	المعز	The Giver of Honour
25	Al Mudil	المذل	The Giver of Dishonor
26	As Sami'	السميع	The All-Hearing
27	Al Basir	البصير	The All-Seeing
28	Al Hakam	الحكم	The Judge; The Ultimate Arbiter
29	Al 'Adl	العدل	The Utterly Just
30	Al Latif	اللطيف	The Kind
31	Al Khabir	الخبير	The All-Aware
32	Al Halim	الحليم	The Forbearer; The Indulgent
33	Al-'Azeemu	العظيم	The Magnificent; The Infinite
34	Al Ghafur	الغفور	The All-Forgiving

35	Ash Shakur	الشكور	The Most Appreciative[1]
36	Al Ali	العلي	The Sublimely Exalted
37	Al Kabir	الكبير	The Great
38	Al Hafiz	الحفيظ	The Preserver; The Protector
39	Al Muqit	المقيت	The Nourisher
40	Al Hasib	الحسيب	The Reckoner
41	Al Jalil	الجليل	The Majestic
42	Al Karim	الكريم	The Bountiful; The Generous
43	Ar Raqib	الرقيب	The Watchful
44	Al Mujib	المجيب	The Responsive; The Answerer
45	Al Wasi'	الواسع	The Vast; The All Encompassing

46	Al Hakim	الحكيم	The Wise
47	Al Wadud	الودود	The Loving; The Kind One
48	Al Majeed	المجيد	The All Glorious
49	Al Ba'ith	الباعث	The Raiser of the Dead
50	Ash Shaheed	الشهيد	The Witness
51	Al Haqq	الحق	The Truth; The Real
52	Al Wakil	الوكيل	The Trustee; The Dependable
53	Al Qawiyy	القوي	The Strong
54	Al Mateen	المتين	The Firm; The Steadfast
55	Al Wali	الولي	The Protecting Friend, Patron, and Supporter
56	Al Hamid	الحميد	The All Praise Worthy

57	Al Muhsi	المحصي	The Accounter; The Numberer of All
58	Al Mubdi	المبدئ	The Producer, Originator, and Initiator of all
59	Al Mu'id	المعيد	The Reinstater Who Brings Back All
60	Al Muhyi	المحيي	The Giver of Life
61	Al Mumit	المميت	The Bringer of Death; The Destroyer
62	Al Hayy	الحي	The Ever Living
63	Al Qayyum	القيوم	The Self Subsisting Sustainer of All
64	Al Waajid	الواجد	The Perceiver; The Finder; The Unfailing
65	Al Maajid	الماجد	The Illustrious; The Magnificent
66	Al Waahid	الواحد	The One; The All Inclusive; The Indivisible

67	Al Ahad	الاحد	The One; The Indivisible
68	As Samad	الصمد	The Everlasting; The Eternal Refuge
69	Al Qaadir	القادر	The All-Capable; The Most Able; The Most Powerful
70	Al Muqtadir	المقتدر	The All Determiner; The Dominant
71	Al Muqaddim	المقدم	The Expediter; He Who Brings Forward
72	Al Mu'akhkhir	المؤخر	The Delayer; He Who Brings Backwards
73	Al Awwal	الأول	The First
74	Al Aakhir	الأخر	The Last
75	Az zhahir	الظاهر	The Manifest; The All Victorious
76	Al Baatin	الباطن	The Hidden; The All Encompassing

77	Al Waali	الوالي	The Patron
78	Al Muta'ali	المتعالي	The Self Exalted
79	Al Barr	البر	The Most Kind and Righteous
80	At Tawwaab	التواب	The Ever-Pardoning, Ever Relenting
81	Al Muntaqim	المنتقم	The Avenger
82	Al 'Afuww	العفو	The Pardoner; The Forgiver
83	Ar Ra'uf	الرؤوف	The Clement; The Compassionate; The All-Pitying
84	Malik Al Mulk	مالك الملك	The Owner of All Sovereignty
85	Zul Jalal wa Al Ikram	ذو الجلال و الإكرام	The Lord of Majesty and Generosity
86	Al Muqsit	المقسط	The Equitable; The Requiter

87	Al Jaami'	الجامع	The Gatherer; The Unifier
88	Al Ghani	الغني	The All Rich; The Independent
89	Al Mughni	المغني	The Enricher; The Emancipator
90	Al Mani'	المانع	The Withholder; The Shielder; The Defender
91	Ad Dharr	الضآر	The Distresser
92	An Nafi'	النافع	The Propitious; The Benefactor
93	An Nur	النور	The Light
94	Al Hadi	الهادي	The Guide
95	Al Badi'i	البديع	Incomparable; The Originator
96	Al Baaqi	الباقي	The Ever Enduring and Immutable
97	Al Waarith	الوارث	The Heir; The Inheritor of All

| 98 | Ar Rashid | الرشيد | The Guide, Infallible Teacher, and Knower |
| 99 | As Saboor | الصبور | The Forbearing; The Patient |

These names are the realities of Allah. They are the characteristics of the most Beautiful Being, the Loving, Compassionate, Sovereign, most Powerful, most Merciful. These names of Allah are not the only names of Allah. These are only the names known and revealed to mankind through
the Quran. In fact there are many more beautiful characteristics not known to mankind. Some that we don't know are known by the Angels, the previous Prophets and Messengers and to certain men of God who are beloved by the most High due to their deeds.

The Divine Nature of Allah is infinite, and unimaginable. Your Lord is the Originator of the heavens, the earth, and all that is in between. And He is also the Originator of Love. Love begins with Him, continues through Him, and eternally exists by Him. Love your Creator enough to forbid what He doesn't Love, and Allah will bestow upon you love. Perhaps that love that Allah envelopes around your entire being, will cause you to love yourself. This love you gain for yourself will then manifest itself around you and spread. Love Allah and Allah will love you.

"Say, to them, O Muhammad, 'If you love Allah, then follow me, Allah will love you, and forgive you your sins.' Allah is Forgiving, most Merciful." Quran 3:31

This is what Islam teaches. Islam teaches, that the One who Created us does not live for a specified time, rather He is eternal. The Lord does not possess any human weaknesses. The One who gives life and death, has never been deprived of existence, and will continue to exist. The One who gives rest, has never fell into the influence of sleep or slumber. Sleep is a state of unawareness, the Almighty is the All-Aware, and Ever-Aware. Sleep is a gift that the Creator bestowed upon mankind. To ever say that the Creator of this universe is in need of rest, will mean that this entire universe will fall off course. This universe is in need of Allah, this universe is in need of the Awareness of its Creator.

"no sleep overtakes Him, nor slumber..." Quran 2:255

The orbit, the sun, the moon; indeed, the Highest is in control of all of these realities. In order for everything in existence to stay on course it would require proper awareness. Thus, Allah is also the Maintainer and Sustainer of this universe. The creation of this world, does not have the capabilities to sustain and maintain itself. As humans, we are not in control of the properties in the atmosphere that cooperate with the functions of our lungs, or the vessels in our blood that are responsible for the beat of our hearts. All of these realities must have an Originator, one who is responsible for its function.

"He is the Originator of all that is in the heavens and the earth..."
Quran

The Almighty Lord, is the most Merciful. The Mercy of Allah can be seen in the Creation of the night and the day. Mankind finds in vast heavens the brilliant sun, its radiant magnanimity and wide scope which covers the entire heavens, useful for their daily endeavors. The absence of the suns brilliance is replaced with darkness. Conveniently mankind looks to the sky once again and finds a radiant lamp giving light and heavens furthermore filled with stars. The lamp serving as a light in the darkness, and the stars positioned in accuracy used as a guiding compass by men. Everything in this universe is created by the Lord and enveloped with His Everlasting Compassion and Mercy. The mercy of Allah can be seen in his messages and revelation to mankind. The Mercy of Allah can be seen in every aspect of the creation, to name each and every circumstance in this universe that exhibits signs of the Merciful nature of the most High will fill entire volumes, and books endlessly.

"Limitless is the Lord in His mercy..." Quran 6:147

The Power and Might of our Lord can be seen the moment a new born takes His first breath. It can be seen the moment the new born gains his first heartbeat in the womb of his mother. It is not the helpless newborn that has the power to form his heart or allow air to escape and return within the fold of his lungs; it is not the power of the newborn to choose its own mother, or be able to create his own mother, rather it is the Compassion of the most Merciful. The Almighty Lord is, the King of all Kings. All Governance, Power, Sovereignty and Might belongs to Him.

A king of this world has limitations while the Original King has no limitations.

What was there before the Universe

Before this universe there was, its Creator — Allāh (الله جَلَّ جَلَالُه). This is the personal and universal name of the Creator of this entire universe. Prophet Muhammād was once asked the following:

"O Allah's Messenger! Where was our Lord before He created the heavens and earth?" He صَلَّى اللهُ عَلَيهِ وَسَلَّم responded: "He was above white clouds – no air was under him, no air was above him, and He created His Throne upon the water."

Reported by Ahmad, 15767. At-Tirmidhee, 3109. Ibn Maajah, 182. The narration was declared authentic by At-Tabaree. Declared hasan by At-Tirmidhee, Adh-Dhahabee and Ibn Taymiyyah. However, Shaikh Al-Albaanee declared it weak in Da'eef Sunan at-Tirmidhee, but Ibn 'Uthaimeen and others considered it authentic, and Allāh جَلَّ جَلَالُه knows best]

"There was Allāh جَلَّ جَلَالُه and nothing else before Him and His Throne was over the water, and He then created the Heavens and the Earth and wrote everything in the Book." (Reference of this Hadith is from Fat-hul-Baaree 6/289)

Allāh جَلَّ جَلَالُه is outside of space and time. He is above this universe, above the heavens and above His throne. While we are in need of the realm of space and held captive by the confines of time – Allāh جَلَّ جَلَالُه is free from

60

the need of time and space. Rather time, is a organized succession that was created by him, to govern the celestial orbit of this universe. We continuously experience our present becoming the past, and entering a future. While the Divine creator is above the need of time. He ﷻ is in the moment. He just, is.

This a classic reason why, when the final revelation (the Qurān) speaks of things that happened in the past – Allāh ﷻ doesn't say: "A long time ago, this is what happened." Rather He ﷻ says, "And remember when…." And mention to them when…" "And remind them of the story of Zacharia…." Even the language and linguistic style of Allāh is free from the confines of time. This shows, that the Qurān is a book that is, in itself outside the realm and capability of this universe. And is a proof, above all other religious teachings that it is the authentic words of the Greatest (Allāh ﷻ).

Who is God?

God took for himself the name" Allah". The name Allah is neither masculine nor feminine. Rather, He is incomparable to any living creature He created. While most Christians I know may argue "God created us in his image." Muslims believe God is nothing like his creation. He is unable to be perceived by any of the senses, since we have no knowledge of the unseen. Among the names He chose for himself includes, the most powerful and the all-knowing; the giver and the taker; the wise and the generous; while He is the most merciful to his creation, He can also be stern in punishment if needed. His attributes and names that are used to praise Him are 99.

To name a few; the Almighty, the Majestic, the Creator, the Forgiver, the Honorable and the Guardian of his creation. Last but not least in the following verse, God describes Himself in great detail "Allah! There is no god but He – the Living, The Self–Subsisting, Eternal. No slumber can seize Him nor sleep. His are all things in the heavens and on earth. Who is there that can intercede In His presence except as He permits? He knows what appears to His creatures before, after or behind them. Nor shall they compass any of his knowledge except as He wills. His throne extends Over the heavens and on earth, and He never feels fatigue in guarding and preserving them, for He is the Most High. The Supreme in glory." [Surah al-Baqarah 2: 255]

His 99 names were revealed to the prophet Mohamed (peace be upon him), and many prophets before that were familiar with his most sublime names. In the English language, Gods name can take many forms. It can become plural like 'gods' or 'goddesses'. However, the name God took for himself 'Allah' cannot be made into a plural form. This indicates that he is unique and no being can reach his status.

> **"Say (O Mohamed), 'He is Allah, the One;**
> **Allah, the Eternal, Absolute;**
> **He begets not, and neither is He begotten;**
> **And there is nothing that can be compared to Him."**

> **Qur'an 112:1-4**

Gods power can be seen through his creation. In fact, the last prophet; Mohamed (peace upon him) encourages Muslims to know themselves in order to know Allah. One should look at the way they were created. God gave us eyes to see, a mouth to speak, hands to use, and feet to be able to walk around. Most importantly he gave us intellect and a mind so that we may reason and use logic. All of these are countless blessings that he is showering us with and in return what do human beings do? We constantly take his words as a jest. We don't realize that this life is only temporary and there is a greater meaning as to why we are here.

63

"Do the people think that they will be left to say, "We believe" and they will not be tried?" 29:2

In the holy Qur'an God encourages human beings in countless verses to use logic and reason, to find out who He is. An example of that would be the verse; *"It is a Book We have sent down to you, full of blessing, so let people of intelligence ponder (liyaddabbaru) its Signs and take heed."* [38:29]

"Will they not then ponder the Qur'an or are there locks upon their hearts?" [Muhammad, 47:24]

In order to understand our Creator, the correct way one must open the Qur'an and read it. One day I was with young children in a Saturday class. One of them asked me a really great question. She said, "How is that a person can die right now where we live and that same second another person is taking their last breath? How does the Angel of Death work so fast?" I told her, "If Allah can cause us to speak, think and contemplate without any problems; and at the other side of the world people are speaking, thinking and contemplating as we are now; What makes you think he can't take the souls of people simultaneously at the same time?

Life on Earth before the Creation of Adam

There is nothing in the Quran or Sunnah to indicate that there were any people living on Earth before Adam (peace be upon him). The reports that speak of this are opinions of mufasireen (Quran commentators) among the sahabah (companions) and tabi'een (successors).

The first opinion states earth was inhabited by the jinn, whom Allah the most High created from fire. The opinion was narrated from most of the mufasireen.

At-Tabari narrated in his Tafseer from Ibn Abbas (rahimahullah) that he said:

"The first ones to dwell on earth were the jinn, and they caused mischief therein, shedding blood and killing one another." It was also narrated by Ar'Rabee' Ibn Anas: "Allah created the angels on Wednesday, and He created the jinn on Thursday and He created Adam on Friday. Then some of the jinn disbelieved, and the angels used tcome down to earth to lead them, and there was bloodshed and corruption on earth." Allah knows best about the reality of this saying, however we know for sure that our father Adam (peace be upon him) was created on Friday, as there are many authentic ahadith that mention this.

Ibn Kathir said in his book Al-Bidayah wa Nihayah: "many scholars of tafseer say that the jinn were created before Adam (peace be upon him), and before them on Earth there were the hinn and the binn, then Allah caused the jinn to prevail over them, so they killed them and expelled them from the earth and inhabited it after them."

The second opinion is that there was no one on earth, jinn or otherwise, before Adam (peace be upon him) At-Tabari narrated this view in his Tafseer from Abd' Ar-Rahman ibn Zayd, who said:

Allah, may He be exalted said to the angels: I want to create a creature on earth and make him a vicegerent, leader (or khilafa) therein. On that day Allah had no creation except the angels, and there were no other creatures on earth.

What was the First thing to be Created?

What really was the first thing to be created? There is a difference among past major scholars on what was created first; the throne or the pen?

Ibn Katheer stated in Al-Bidaayah wan-Nihaayah (vol. 1, p. 8) in summary: There is some differing regarding what was created first, so some say: Allaah created the Pen (Al-Qalam) . However, that which the majority of the Scholars are upon is that the Throne (Al-'Arsh) preceded the creation of the pen

Argument One the Throne was first (Majority Agreement)

The first thing that Allāh ﷻ created of the things that are known to us was His Throne, which He rose over after He created the heavens, as Allah says: "And He it is Who has created the heavens and the earth in six Days and His Throne was on the water, that He might try which of you is the best in deeds" — Qurān 11:7

An authentic hadith of `Imraan Ibn Husayn (رضي الله عنه) states that Allah's Messenger ﷺ said:

"There was Allah ﷻ and nothing else before Him and His Throne was over the water, and then He created the Heavens and the Earth and wrote everything in the Book." — Saheeh Bukhari 6982, 3192

Abdullaah Ibn `Amr Ibn Al-`Aas narrated from the Messenger ﷺ: " Allāh wrote the decree of all of creation 50,000 years before the creation of the heavens and the earth. And His Throne was over the water." — Muslim, 2653

So they understand the narration, 'the first thing that Allāh created was the Pen' to truly mean, 'the first thing he created in the beginning of our universe (not outside of it)'

Argument Two the Pen was first
(Minority Consensus)

Some say, Allāh ﷻ created the Pen (Al-Qalam) before all of these things, and that was the preference of Ibn Jareer, and Ibn Jawze. Ibn Jareer said: "And after the Pen it was the creation of the fine clouds."

They also use as proof of the hadith narrated by: Ubadah Ibn Saamit (رضي الله عنه) from the Messenger (): "Indeed the first thing that Allāh created was the Pen." [Ahmad 23197. Abu Dawud, 4700. At-Tirmidhi, 2155]

In summary: the minority of scholars believe that the pen was created first. That it was created way before the creation of our universe, and outside of it. While the majority argue: that the Hadith saying the pen was first – meant that it was simply the first thing created after the universe came into existence. And that the Qurān verse in Surah Hud proves the throne was first, before the creation of the universe.

Creation of the Universe

One example of the harmony between the Qur'an and modern science is the subject of the age of the universe. Cosmologists estimate the age of the universe as 16^{-17}billion years. The Qur'an states that the entire universe was created in six days. These two-time frames, which may seem contradictory, are actually surprisingly compatible. In fact, both these figures concerning the age of the universe are correct. In other words, the universe was created in six days, as revealed in the Qur'an, and this period corresponds to 16-17 billion years in the way that we experience time.

In 1915 Einstein proposed that time was relative, that the passage of time altered according to space, the speed of the person travelling and the force of gravity at that moment. Bearing in mind these differences in the passage of time, the period of time in which the universe was created as revealed in seven different verses of the Qur'an is actually highly compatible with scientists' estimations. The six-day period revealed in the Qur'an can be thought of as six periods. Because, taking into account the relativity of time, a "day" refers only to a 24-hour period experienced on Earth under current conditions.

Elsewhere in the universe, however, at another time and under other conditions, a "day" could refer to a much longer period of time. Indeed, the word "*ayyamin*" in the period of six days (*sittati ayyamin*) in these verses (Qur'an 32:4, 10:3, 11:7, 25:59, 57:4, 50:38, and 7:54) means not only "days," but also "age, period, moment, term."

In the first period of the universe, the passage of time took place much faster than that with which we are familiar today. The reason for this is that, at the moment of the Big Bang, our universe was compressed into a very small point. The expansion of the universe and increase in its volume ever since the moment of that explosion has extended the borders of the universe to millions of light years. Indeed, the stretching of space ever since that moment has had very important ramifications for universal time.

The energy at the moment of the Big Bang slowed down the flow of time 10^{12} (one million) times. When the universe was created the speed of universal time was higher up to a million times, as time is experienced today. In other words, **a million minutes on Earth is the equivalent of just one minute in universal time**.

When a six-day period of time is calculated according to the relativity of time, it equates to six million (six trillion) days. That is because universal time flows a million times faster than time on Earth. Calculated in terms of years, 6 trillion days equates to approximately 16.427 billion years. This is within the estimated range for the age of the universe.

6,000,000,000,000 days/365.25 = 16.427104723 billion years

On the other hand, each of the six days of creation equates to very different periods, as we perceive time. The reason for this is that the speed of the passage of time declines in proportion to the expansion of the universe. Ever since the Big Bang, as the size of the universe doubled, so the passage of time halved. As the universe grew, the speed at which the universe doubled increasingly slowed down. This rate of expansion is a scientific fact acknowledged the world over and described in the text book *The Fundamentals of Physical Cosmology.*

When we calculate every day of creation in terms of Earth time, the following situation emerges:

Looked at from the moment when time began, the first day of creation (first phase) lasted 24 hours. This period, however, is the equivalent of 8 billion years in Earth terms.
The second day of creation (second phase) lasted 24 hours. This, however, lasted half as long, in our terms, as the preceding day, in other words 4 billion years.
The third day (third phase) lasted half as long as the second day, in other words 2 billion years.
The fourth day (fourth phase) lasted 1 billion years.
The fifth day (fifth phase) lasted 500 million years.
And the sixth day (sixth phase) lasted 250 million years.
Conclusion: **When the six days of creation, in other words the six phases, are added together in Earth terms, the resulting figure is 15 billion 750 million years. This figure displays an enormous parallel with modern-day estimations.**

This conclusion is one of the facts revealed by 21st century science. Science has once again confirmed a fact revealed in the Qur'an 1,400 years ago. This harmony between the Qur'an and some observations recently made in science is one of the miraculous proofs that the Qur'an is the revelation of Allah, the Creator, the Omniscient."

The Big Bang

How did the existence of the universe come about? What we know until recently is that the universe is about 13.8 billion years old and earth is about 4.54 billion years old. The question is how do scientists figure out how to calculate the exact numerical value of earths existence? Well, to put it simply earth's age is studied by scientists who take back selected rocks to a laboratory. Those very rocks are tested for elements of radioactive isotopes. The reason why radioactive isotopes play a great role in determining the age of the universe is because they are particles that constantly change within the rock. Each and every time the rocks form there are elements within them go through a cycle of decaying; which scientists call half- life. Once one radioactive particle decays the next non-radioactive particle forms and the cycle keeps on going and never stops. Some of the rocks have very lengthy radioactive particles that don't decay until after millions of years. Scientists observe the measurement of each given element and take the ratio of a certain rocks given numerical value. They then compare it with the numerical existence of other rocks and meteorites. It is because of this cycle of non-radioactive and radioactive elements increasing and decreasing in percentage within a rock for such a long time that scientists can determine the exact age of the rock.

With so many of these studies being conducted, researched, and analyzed around the world; scientists who work close together informed one another of their findings and concluded their data with the average numerical value of earths existence and the universe as a whole. From many observations made by scientists of all backgrounds and experiences, the universe first initiated through one main event. This event is known through the world of science as the 'Big Bang'. It is a theory that has been studied, reviewed, and debated for a very long time. However, the majority of scientists agree that it was an occurrence that took place before the existence of this universe. Even with the world of science and technology advancing to such a high degree, it is sometimes difficult for those who study the history of this universe to make an inference on its existence. In science precision and accuracy matter because if one piece of data is off then the rest of the study will go downhill; which can lead to wrong data and well, wrong beliefs. Considering how enormous this universe is it's easy to understand that it must have be an excruciating amount of studies that were conducted over the past years to put all final conclusions to rest. It also makes sense that the all of the noble and hard work put into the studies of this universe must have been hard since, there are over 200 billion stars in the galaxy, and over hundreds of billions of galaxies.

So, what is the explanation of the Big Bang theory that the majority of scientists have agreed on? This theory states that the universe first started with a small singularity, then inflated over the next 13.8 billion years to the cosmos that we know today.

It was this moment that Allah describes in the Quran, in Surah or Chapter Fussilat, and Fussilat means (Explained in Detail). Read the below verses in detail, it is a description of the creation of this universe, and see for yourself how this matches the theory of how the world started, it begins:

> In the Name of God, the most Compassionate the Most Merciful
> Ha, Meem (these are letters whose initials are only known to God)
> This is a revelation from the Entirely Merciful, the Especially Merciful
> A Book whose verses have been detailed, an Arabic Quran for a people
> who know

As a giver of good tidings and a warner; but most of them turn away, so they do not hear
And they say, "Our hearts are with coverings from which you invite us, and in our ears deafness, and between us and you is a partition, so work, indeed, we are working

Say to them, O Muhammad, "I am only a man like you to whom it has been revealed that your god is but one God; so, take a straight course to Him and seek His forgiveness." And woe to those who associate others with Allah

Those who do not give zakah (charity), and in the Hereafter, they are disbelievers
Indeed, those who believe and do righteous deeds – for them is a reward uninterrupted

And the verses continue (this is the part I want you to pay attention to):

"Say, 'do you indeed disbelieve in He who created the earth in two days and attribute to Him equals? That is the Lord of the worlds.

And He placed on the earth firmly set mountains over its surface, and He blessed it and determined therein its creature's sustenance in four days without distinction – for the information of those who ask

Then He directed Himself to the heaven while it was smoke and said to
it and to the earth '
come into being willingly or by compulsion.' They said, 'we come
willingly."

And He completed them as seven heavens within two days and inspired
in each heaven its command. And We adorned the nearest heaven with
lamps and as a protection. That is the determination of the Exalted in
Might, the Knowing."

The above verses are from Surah Fussilat, Chapter 41 in the Quran. It is
the fact that the initial stage of the universe is described as smoke that
is very intriguing, and something that we should pay attention to.

In current studies scholars and academics in the field of science relay
how over hundreds of thousands of years after the big bang, the
universe was mostly a cloud like, smoke filled chamber. This smokey
chamber is described as a place where light could not escape. It was by
the time the universe celebrated its billionth birthday that the smoke,
which was mostly hydrogen that was trapping gas, cleared completely.
This moment is when the light within it, like the stars and galaxies
started to become visible.

In the above verses the most High, explains how He has positioned His gaze towards the smoke, and expressed for it to either come willingly or unwillingly. This form of creation immediately obeyed God, as its nature (the nature it was created for), was to follow the natural order of the universe that it was given. The moment that the gaze of the Creator was directed towards this smoke, is when all formations of the stars and galaxies began to appear and expand.

Allah the most High, also says of the steady expansion of the universe:

"And the heaven, We have built with might, and We are steadily expanding it." Quran 51:47

Current observation from the scientific community points to the definite expansion of the universe. The expansion of the universe is described as the increasing distance between two points. These points are described as gravitationally position parts that extend overtime, this means that the stars and galaxies surrounding us, including our sun and planet are moving further and further away from us.

It is important to note that the observation of the scientific community does not hold as much weight, when compared to the Words of God. For as long as a human intends to understand the universe, there will always be shortcomings, mistakes, or the inability to fully comprehend the scope of the universe. There is always so much more to learn. Hence, the reason why the Big Bang Theory, is just a theory and not an established fact. It is very interesting though how close this theory is to what Allah describes in the Quran. These verses were revealed way before the establishment of the big bang theory.

After the Big Bang

When the universe was positioned, and every part of creation was given their commands and orders, there are two important occasions that occurred that every Muslim should know. The first occasion is known as the covenant between Allah and humankind. This covenant is mentioned in surah Al-Araf.

THE COVENANT BETWEEN ALLĀH AND MANKIND (SURAH AL-A'RAF)

Did you know:

During the time of Prophet Muhammād ﷺ. The Jewish leaders would present to him certain questions that he must answer; in order to prove the legitimacy of his prophet-hood. There were many questions that they asked. Every time they asked him, Allāh ﷻ would instantly reveal to them the answer, in accurate detail. Each verse would begin, "...Tell them O Prophet..."

On many occasions, they accepted Islam due to how detailed and historically correct the answers were. They thought, a man like Muhammād ﷺ, an Arab, could not be knowledgeable about our long lost history.

Once they asked him about the Soul. This was the only question, they asked, that did not get a detailed response. Allāh ﷻ revealed, "...And they ask you about the soul, tell them, 'this is a matter only for Allāh." Qurān () This meant, no matter how detailed the answer, they can never imagine or understand the nature of the soul. Thus, they should leave this matter to Allāh ﷻ

When Allāh ﷻ first created our souls, he gathered the soul of every human (during عالم الغيب – the world of the unseen).

Our souls were presented with two promises. A Covenant and a Trust from Allāh ﷻ. We don't remember these occasions in our active conscious. But every human has something called the Fitrah, (like an innate GPS) that allows us to remember.

Fitrah is the innate nature that drives human beings to worship. Once Allāh ﷻ presented the Covenant and the Trust to every soul, the Fitrah to worship Him and to Submit to His Will was activated in every human. This means even if you don't worship Allāh ﷻ, you are actively submitting to His will. How? By breathing. By your heartbeat. By the very blood that flows through your body. You have no choice but to follow the natural order, the natural laws of the universe

The Trust Offered to the Universe

In the beginning of time, there was a trust that was offered to the world. This was stated in surah Al-Ahzab.

In this verse God Almighty states:

"We did indeed offer the Trust (amanah) to the Heavens and the Earth and the Mountains: but they refused to undertake it, being afraid thereof: but man undertook it― he was indeed unjust and ignorant." Surah Al-Ahzab verse 72

Think of this like a document, containing a huge offer. However, this offer like many others in the world comes with pros and cons. Allah offered this *amana*, or trust to every single part of creation. The sun, the moon, the stars, the sky, the heavens, the sea, the mountains, and everything in between. This offer was also proposed to the angels, and humans.

Allah states that this offer was not accepted by every other part of creation, except humans. In this verse, human souls are described as being "ignorant" or unknowing, of the full scope that this offer contains. This offer was "free will". This means whichever part of creation accepts this offer, they would be granted the full rights and ability to choose between good and bad, and lead their own path in life.

If we closely observe life, we notice that nature follows the natural order of this universe. The orbits all follow a particular routine, the sun rises and sets according to a specific time, day and night alternate as they should (usually unless an eclipse occurs), the ocean refrains from spilling out into the land (usually, unless God ordains via hurricanes/floods), the angels all follow the commands of God instantly, the clouds, and the mountains remain over the earth with firm loyalty, not crushing its inhabitants. The main point is there is numerical precision and perfection behind nature because they all go with the flow, and obey the commands of God.

Then there are humans, who do not have that precision and balance because we were bestowed with this trust (amana) the moment we accepted it. We were given free will. The ability to do as we please, and be the captains of our own destiny, that God created.

The Prescribed Scrolls, Free Will, and Destiny

It has been emphasized that the friends and close companions of our beloved Prophet Mohamed were once arguing and debating the concept of Al-Qadar. After the Prophet overheard them he emphasized that this is not an affair that should be prolonged unnecessarily. He reminded them that communities before them have been destroyed because of this topic.

Nonetheless, because of Allah's never-ending grace and ever-existing supremacy this subject has been one in which the scholars aforetime have discussed and studied for many years. Ibn Taymiyyah, Ibn Al-Qayyim, Shafi3i, Abu-Hanifa, Muslim, and several others have contributed to this topic accompanied with the true words of the most Merciful, and the authentic and trustworthy sayings of HabeebuAllah Mohamed (s). With that mentioned all of the below information has been directly summarized from what is known in the Qur'an and what we know from the words of our beloved, messenger Mohamed (s). Belief in Al-Qadar is one of the pillars of Eman. Without this pillar, a person is not a true believer. So, what is *Al-Qada Wal Qadar*? Linguistic definitions: **Al-Qadar:** It is Allah's complete Knowledge, the fact that Allah knows everything. It is in His Divine Nature to know everything that occurred in the past in complete detail, the present in its absolute perfection, and all that will occur in the future. The fact that Allah (swt) is the All-Knowing but the most organized; he has recorded everything that was and will be in the Prescribed Scrolls which are written above the highest heavens. This proves the fact that Allah has written all things before their initial existence. **Al-Qadar:** The creation of all things by Allah's Will. **The Pillars of Al-Qadar.** *The Knowledge of Allah;* The fact that Allah knows all things… are explained to us in the Qur'an. "Verily, Allah is the All-Knowing over everything." [8:75

The Written Knowledge of Allah;

The fact that Allah has written everything above the highest heavens, in a protected scroll that only He has access to is explained to us in the Qur'an.
"Do you not know that Allah knows all that is in the Heavens and all that is on earth? Verily, it is all in the Book, Verily! That is easy for Allah." [22:70]

The Will of Allah

At the same time, Allah is the decision maker in this world, the ultimate leader and the King of all Kings. Every situation will be initiated under

His complete command. Since He is the Creator of this universe and is the most knowledgeable on every aspect of this universe it only makes sense that Allah does what he Wills according to His own divine Wisdom...

"If Allah willed He would have made you one nation, but that He may test you in what He has given you..." [5:48]

Al-Amr- The Command

When Allah Wills a thing to happen, it doesn't happen in a long process. It also doesn't take long for it to happen; since Allah is the most Powerful and the most Sovereign it only takes Him a simple word, "Be" and everything miraculously happens the way He ordains it to be...

"Verily, His command, when He intends a thing, is only that He says to it, "Be" and it is..." [36:82]

Al-Khaliq- The Creator

Lastly, the greatest Will that Allah has ordained was the existence of the creation. The fact that He has created, shows that Allah's Will is infinitely Powerful. This whole universe is a mirage of how Powerful and Al-Mighty Allah's commands are. It only took Him one word, and

it all came into existence…the way He wanted it to. This aspect of
Allah's characteristics alone shows us how extremely Powerful He is.

"Verily, Allah is the creator of everything…" [39:62]

All creation falls under two different categories; good (al-khayr wal
hasanah) and bad (alshar wal-sayi'ah)

*"Wherever you may be, death will overtake you even if you are in the
fortresses built up strong and high" And if some good reaches them,
they say, "This is from Allah," but if some evil befalls them, they say,
"This is from you Muhammed." Say: "Allah things are from Allah,"
so what is wrong with these people that they fail to understand any
word? Whatever good reaches you, is from Allah, but whatever evil
befalls you, is due to your own self. And We have sent you O
Muhammed, as a Messenger to mankind, and Allah is Sufficient as a
Witness." [4:78-79]*

In the first part of this verse Allah says that all good and all bad comes
from Him. Then Allah says in the last part of the verse; whatever good
reaches us is from Him, and whatever evil befalls us is due to our own
selves.

So, what does this mean? To sum it all up, all good and bad are from Allah. Allah is the Creator of both of these aspects. However, good and evil happen to us based on our own actions. If we do good Allah (swt) will haste to swiftly reward us with good immediately. Likewise, if we do bad, then Allah will allow for evil to reach us from our own surroundings. It is important to know that good and bad are both phenomenon's that Allah has created.

Regardless, it is substantial to understand that Allah is not unfair…if we do good Allah will give us good. If we do bad, Allah will allow for bad to reach us; and this will all happen because it was our own *choice*. This means that evil never comes from Allah. Evil only comes from the creation. Allah (swt) is the originator of all things good; it is the creation of Allah that has the choice to stick to the good or transform it to evil, all due to their own *nafs* or selves. The reason why Allah has allowed for evil to become the opposite of good, is because Allah (swt) has decreed and promised that every human being has the ability to choose on their own. Whether they choose to stick to the purity of their own soul, since birth or avert from that path and choose evil is all a click away.

This is because Allah does not force an individual to be a certain way; the categories of good and evil exist to give the human being alternatives to choose from. The existence of good and evil is an open sea, in which the mind and intellect of human has the ability to swim in all through their own actions. And Allah even says this in the Qur'an in Surat Al-Mulk;

"He who has created death and life, so that He might test you and show which of you will be best in conduct, and make you realize that He alone is the Al-mighty, truly Forgiving." [67:2]

So, one may ask; what about poverty? what about wars? what about violence, crimes, hatred, and the injustice that is occurring all around the world.

Many absentmindedly and foolishly blame God for all of these catastrophe's going on around the world. Little do they know that, all of the evil happening in this world is happening because humans choose for it to continue to happen. If the whole mankind wanted poverty to end, they would have collectively contributed the little they have in order to increase the economy of all of the impoverished countries around the world.

If the whole of mankind wanted war, violence, crimes, and hatred to come to an end they would learn to collectively promote peace, stability, justice, fairness, and love around the world. Until those who have power turn the other check with all of the injustice plaguing the world, then they will be allowing for evil to prevail in this world for as long as they wish. The fact that there are humans that have the ability to change so much around themselves and influence good around the world; yet they ignore what is around them at all costs, shows that evil is prevalent because there isn't enough attempt on mankind's part to correct it.

Allah on the other hand, is silently watching from above giving humans the choice to stand up against evil amongst themselves once and for all; by changing what's within themselves one by one. He is also all-aware of all of the tragedies, and endless crimes that human beings choose to commit. Thus, Allah rewards the evil with what they deserve in this world and in the life to come; and He rewards the righteous as they deserve in this world and in the life to come.

So, what is the wisdom behind the existence of calamities and sinfulness?

All of the evil occurring in this world are all because either Allah is testing those He wishes to test. It could be that He is punishing those who fairly deserve punishment, or perhaps Allah is giving those who are in the midst of committing evil a chance to turn back and repent; a chance to see their wrong doings by having a taste of their own medicine. It can even be a combination of any of the aforementioned points. As we have seen scenes from the Qur'an describing the tribes of Aa'd and Thamud; many of the "natural disasters", earthquakes, hurricanes, and tornadoes are signs from God to show mankind a little of what He is capable of. A demonstration of his complete Power and Sovereign attributes. The thing is, evil comes from mankind's own

choices and decisions and Allah is just and fair so He gives each group what they deserve.
Allah says to mankind;

> *"Alif. Lam. Meem. Do people think that they will be left alone because they say; "We believe," and will not be tested." [29;1-2]*

Calamities and tests come from Tarbiah and Ta'deeb; Tests and Trials that are passed by Allah to give humans a chance to contemplate on the calamities of others or even learn a lesson from them.

> **"And indeed, We punished the people of Fir'awn (Pharoah) with years of drought and shortness of fruits (crops, etc....) that they might remember and take heed." [7:130]**

Evil befalls humans because of their own selves and does not come from God. In other words whoever works evil will reap what he sows, and will be given what he deserves sooner or later; and this has always been a universal rule of the Lord of the Worlds;

> *"It will not be in accordance with your desires (Muslims), nor those of the people of the Scripture (Jews and Christians), whosoever works evil, will have the recompense thereof, and he will not find any protector or helper besides Allah." [4:123]*

Mankind at large is spoiled with what we call, "time". Each human is gifted with an appointed term, in which Allah patiently waits and watches until they turn back, correct themselves, or repent. It is in the ability within one's own intellect that they will realize sooner or later, that there must be something about this world that has a purpose. At that point Allah either shows them signs from all over, for them to ponder, reflect, and contemplate on what their ultimate reason for living is. Allah is not neglectful of His creation, rather the creation has tendencies to be neglectful of their ever-Merciful Lord.

So, which of these logical possibilities exist in Allah's creation?

1) Either the creation is 100% good
2) There is more good than bad in the creation
3) Bad and good in the creation is equal
4) There is more bad than good in the creation
5) And finally, the creation is 100% bad

First off, there is only one creation of Allah out there that is 100% good as a whole; they are the Angels of Allah. There is also heaven, and the Prophets, Messengers and good people that can be easily considered in this category. So, this can be checked off. There is good in the creation.

There is more good than bad in the creation. Is there more good than bad in creation? The creation of Allah has the possibility to have more good than bad.

Is bad and good in the creation equal? No. It is not…if you think you can name two factors or creations of Allah that are equal in their good and bad, then attempt to name one.

There is more bad than good in creation. No. Many people would say that alcohol has more bad than good; because of the verse in Surah Al-Baqara; however, Alcohol is not directly created by Allah. Allah (swt) gave us the properties of the Alcohol. He has given us grapes. But, who are the ones who crush the grapes and dry them in order to make it out of Alcohol? Humans.

Although Allah is the originator and creator of all of the properties in alcohol; humans are the ones who make it the intoxicant and addictive that it is today; with their own actions. So no, there is nothing in the creation of Allah that has more bad than good.

Finally, is there anything in the creation that is 100% bad? No. Many people would say yes; they would say that the Shaytan is 100%bad. The Shaytan is the Creation of Allah (swt); when he was originally created by Allah he was not bad. He was pure and he started off good.

This means that when he was first created by Allah; Allah (swt) in his Divine and good intentions, wished to create something good. Later on, it would be up to the Shaytan to continue being good or stray from that path due to his own decisions and choices. And, we all know it was because of his arrogance that he strayed from the path of Allah. So, what does this mean? This means, when Allah originally creates something.... the thing that He creates does not start off as 100% bad. It starts off as pure, and good...and it is due to the circumstances of an individual's own choices that they stray from that path.

So, using this four-step logic, what can we conclude?

We can easily conclude that there are things in the creation of Allah that are 100% good, there are also things in the creation of Allah that have more good than bad. Lastly there is nothing in the creation of Allah that starts off having more bad than good, and there is nothing in the creation of Allah that starts off 100% bad. Due to this logic, we now see that Allah is the Creator of all things good, and the choices and decisions of His creation are what drive them to evil. Thus, most evil is directly linked to human action, and there is no absolute evil. There is also nothing in the world that is born or created evil; (even the Shaytan), there is no inherent evil, and all evil is adventitious.

That being said; what are the benefits of calamities for the Muslim, or the believer in God?

1) Through every calamity that befalls a person due to a test from Allah. The most Merciful will raise their level and status in this life and in the after-life. We see this in many scenes in the Qur'an. Especially in the story of Prophet Yusuf (a).

2) For any good a person was going to do, and hardship befalls him so that he is prevented from doing it, Allah will still reward him abundantly.

3) There is a promise from Allah that a person who suffers any extreme hardship; they will be recompensed with good in this life and greatly rewarded in the life to come. Allah's Will (Mashee'ah) and Wisdom (Hikmah) are the reason behind all of His actions. Will and Wisdom are based on His Knowledge.

"But you cannot will, unless Allah wills, Verily Allah is the Lord of the Worlds." Qur'an

Our actions are divided into two categories; by choice, and by no choice.

1) Things that are our choice, our daily activities, intentions, deeds, thoughts, beliefs, ways, and decisions.

2) Things that are not our choice; where we originally come from, our race, ethnicity, facial features, height, parents, eye color, etc.

All of our characteristics that involve no choice are attributed to Allah directly and completely. As for matter of choice, Allah is th source of our actions but we are the ones performing the actions on our own precaution and gifted intellect from the Almighty. At-Tawfeeq and Al-Khuldaan

"...and my (tawfeeq) guidance cannot come except from Allah, in Him I trust and unto Him I repent." [11:88]

"...then when you have taken a decision, put your trust in Allah, certainly, Allah loves those who put their trust in Him. If Allah helps you, none can overcome you; and if He forsakes you (yakhdhulkum), who is there after Him that can help you? And in Allah (alone) let believers put their trust." [3:159-160]

Al-hidayah is guidance, and al-khuldan means to be left to your own self. Hidayah can be guidance that is worldly or religious; it can be worldly knowledge and guidance or religious guidance. Allah gives both of these factors to who he wishes to give it to. Hidayah or guidance can be divided into two categories

1) Religious Guidance;

a) Hidayat-Albayan or Al-Irshad (guidance through education, explanation, or information)

b) Hidayat-Altawfeeq (guidance through favor, assistance, or granting success)

The Prophets and Messengers of Allah were gifted with both; and it may be throughout the creation of Allah…that Allah gifts both or one out of the two to whom he wishes. On the other Al-Khuldan is when Allah shows so many signs to an individual and exceeds in giving the individual many chances to repent, chance, or come back to Allah…and they utterly refuse each and every time; Allah makes the final will to leave the individual alone and allow them to continue the way they are. This is actually the worst position that a human can be in; because their source of peace, protection, hope, and aspiration will let them go once and for all; that is…of course unless they turn back to the most Merciful.

Can Al-Qadar be Changed?

There are two scrolls where the destiny of humans is written:

1) Al-Lawhul-Mahfudh the Prescribed Tablet or Safe Tablet; or Prescribed Scrolls or sometimes called Umm Al-Kitab (The Mother of all books)

2) The Scrolls with the Angels
The Prescribed Scrolls written atop the highest heavens is with Allah (swt) and not one individual has access to it; except Allah. In it are the details of this world and beyond in the most precise and accurate details and description. Every leaf on the barks of the trees around the world, to the hair strands on the scalp of one's skull, to the minute details of the daily lives of the creation of Allah (swt). Nothing in it changes, everything in it is determined and absolute. All that has happened, all

that is happening, and all that is yet to come are recorded by Allah (swt) and kept in what is called; Alawahul-Mahfudh.

The scrolls with the Angels also have the records of all things. However, the scrolls with the Angels is not the same as the one with Almighty. The ones that are with Angels of Allah, are not determined and absolute. It may be that a person makes duaa to be protected from all harm one day and on that day, it was written for them on the tablet of the angels; that they would have gotten hurt. However, because that individual made duaa to Allah (swt); Allah will command the Angels to erase what harm would have befallen that person and order for Him to protected. Note, this is just an example. The Scrolls with the Angels can be changed, due to the duaa and supplication of a given individual. However, the recorded book with Allah is perfect, and does not need to be changed.

So, with all of this known, do humans have a choice?

Obviously, we have the choice to do whatever we wish. It is because Allah created all of the potential possibilities of good and bad, and laid it out for us that we have the ultimate choice to choose what we want. In addition, Allah has gifted us with fresh intellect, and sound knowledge to be able to discern between what is evil and what is good. That alone should show that the choice lies within our own grasp.

Likewise, Allah did not burden us with the knowledge of the future…and because we do not know all that will happen we have the immediate comfort of choosing our actions anyway we wish. Imagine knowing the details of our futures. Then, every human in the world would rush to be a certain way or prevent a certain factor in their lives, or even live with fear due to the simple knowledge of knowing the future. It is because we live in the present and see what unfolds moment by moment, that our actions are performed by our own selves accordingly. And Allah is the most Wise.

What are the benefits of Belief in Al-Qadar?

1) A peace of mind; one will know that all things will happen according to Allah and that the burden of the future is lifted off of your shoulder.

2) Your concern will not be so much with the past or the future. Your main concern is your present actions.

3) It gives you the will power and determination to go forward in the way of Allah.

4) It teaches you to be humble and honest.

5) Leads to total dependence upon Allah. You take precautions; do as much as you can and then depend upon H

Part 2: The First Creations on Earth

When Allah Created Paradise and Hell

Allah sent Angel Jibreel (Gabriel) peace be upon him to Paradise and said: 'look at it and at what I have prepared for its people therein.' So, he went and looked at it. When he returned he said, 'By your glory, no one will hear of it but he will enter it.' Then Allah commanded that is should be surrounded with difficult things. The most High said, 'Go back,' He went back and saw that it was surrounded with difficult things. Angel Gabriel came back and said, 'By your Glory, I am afraid that no one will enter it.' Allah said, 'Go and look at Hell, see what I have prepared for its people therein,' He saw parts of it consuming other parts. He came back and said, 'By your Glory, no one who hears of it will enter it,' So Allah commanded that it should be surrounded with desires. Then he said, 'God back to it,' So he returned and said, 'By your Glory, I am afraid that no one will be saved from it and that all will enter it." Sahih Bukhari

The Angels

Fact: The Angels are created out of light and the oldest angel is Angel Gabriel.

"All praise is due to Allah who created the heavens and the earth, and the angels – messengers with wings two or three or four. He adds to Creation as He pleases: for Allah has power over all things." Quran 35:1

Belief in angels is one of the six pillars of belief or faith. Whoever does not believe in any of these pillars is not a believer (mumin).

Where are they? Angels are a part of "the world of the unseen" which we cannot envision or comprehended. They are created from light.

When were they created? There is no knowledge of precisely when they were created. But they were created before mankind for certain, Allah said: "behold, your Lord said to the angels: I will create a vicegerent on earth,'" [2:30] The fact that Allah told them od His intention to create humanity indicates they already existed.

Their size? "O you who believe! Save yourselves and your families from a Fire whose fuel is men and stones, over which are (appointed) angels stern and severe, who flinch not (from executing) the commands they receive from Allah, but do (precisely) what they are commanded.

The greatest of all the angels? He is Jibreel. "He had six hundred wings, each of which covered the horizon. There fell from his winfs jewels, pearls, and rubies, only Allah knows about them." Hadith Hassan –

I saw Jibreel descending from heaven, and his great size filled the space between heaven and earth." [Muslim]

They have wings: Quran 35:1 and they are immense in beauty which is stated in the Quran 53: 5-6
"He [Muhammad], has been taught by the one Mighty in Power, Dhoo Mirrah (which means free from any defect in body and mind), then he rose and became stable." Quran 53: 5-6

Ibn Abbas said: "Dhoo Mirrah means that he has a beautiful appearance." Qatadah said: "He is tall and beautiful."

They are not all one size or status; there are differences between them just as there are differences in their virtue. It is stated in a Sahih Hadith that the best angels were those present at Badr. And the best group of Muslims were the ones present at Badr.

They do not eat or drink. And this is indicated in the story of Abraham when the angels visited him in the form of men. He offered them food, and they declined. This caused Abraham (alayhi salam) to become afraid. Because people in his time did not refuse food when offered. They said, "…fear not we are messengers from your Lord." And that's when he knew they were angels.

The idea in mainstream society today, about angels is very different from how they really are. Angels are not timid small babies, with halos over their heads. Angels are far from what many people assume in today's world. They are very strong and powerful, and they are not a sight that humans can even handle, because of how terrifyingly magnificent that they have been created.

The Nature of the Angels

Before I take you on the journey of the prophets sent by God, we must first understand who Gabriel (peace be upon him) was. In order to understand Gabriel; we must first understand Angels, because Gabriel is an Angel.

In Islam, Angels are not given the choice of will, like mankind was. It is not in their nature to be able to choose from right and wrong. Thus, they only answer to the Ultimate Commander and Chief; God Almighty. They do what they are told, never question God, and go about their way. They have a love, desire and want to worship God Almighty like we have the need to breath. Made of pure light, these fascinating entities always fascinated me.

They are large giant-like creatures; in fact, God describes them in the Qur'an as following:

**"All praise is due to Allah Creator of the
heavens and the earth, who made the angels;
messengers having wings, two**

or three or four. He increases in creation what He wills. Indeed,
Allah is over all things competent." 35:1

Angels are the messengers of God. They are diligent in their work, and
carry out all important commands of the universe by the will of God.
Through the Power of God; they are noble entities, who are very
perceptive, astute and intelligent. Unlike human beings, they do what
they are told and never question the logical reasoning behind the
commands of their Lord.

There are many Angels in this universe. There are tens of thousands of
Angels in this entire universe. The prophet Muhammed (peace be upon
him) mentioned that they are so much in number, that one wouldn't
find a space of two fingers in the heavens were an angel isn't
prostrating to God Almighty, or glorifying him through praises.

Angels being made out of light, are so fast. So, fast that they are in fact
the epitome of the speed of light. Angels are low density creatures. God
created them originally from light. They move at any speed from zero
up to the speed of light. It is the angels who carry out God's orders.
Those angels take their orders from a Preserved Tablet somewhere in
outer space, and not from God's Throne. That is because God in his
ultimate sublime attributes, is unreachable and above all of his creation.

Thus, the Angels commute to and from this Preserved Tablet to get their orders from God. In the following verse, the Quran describes how angels travel when they commute to and from this Tablet. And the speed at which they commute to and from this Tablet turned out to be the known as speed of light:

"It is Allah who rules the cosmic affair from the heavens to the Earth. Then this affair travels to Him a distance in one day, at a measure of one thousand years of what you count." Qur'an 32:5

It is the angels who carry out these orders. People back then didn't measure the distance of traveling in kilometers nor in miles but rather by how much time they needed to walk. For example, a village three days away meant a distance equivalent to walking for three days; ten days away meant a distance equivalent to walking for ten days.

However, in this verse the Quran specifies 1000 years of what they counted; not what they walked. So, what does the Qur'an mean, "...by what they counted." Looking closely at this verse one will see that it is referring to the calendar that was used. Back then people followed the lunar calendar. The lunar calendar counted twelve lunar months each year.

Since it is lunar, these months are related to the moon and not the sun. Which is the reason why in 1 day angels will travel a distance of 1000 years of what they counted.

What did they count? They counted the moon. So, if they counted the moon this means the verse is referring to the 12 months in the lunar calendar. If God said the angels travel a distance of 1000 years then, 12 months multiplied by 1000 will calculate up to 12,000. The moon travels at about 12,000 lunar orbits. If this is so, then God is comparing how fast the moon travels to how fast the Angels are in one day.

To break it down into simple terms; the Angels travel in 12,000 lunar orbits in ONE day. That is faster than you can finish blinking! That being said, these beings are capable of so much; because of the way God the most Powerful has created them, they are very strong.

Angels are beyond our imagination. Such excellent beings they are, and how determined and steadfast they are in obeying the command of God. Made out of bright light, I can only *imagine* how amazing they look.

Many people see Angels as good forces of nature, hologram images, or illusions. In America and even across the world, most people portray Angels as chubby cute babies, or beautiful and handsome youth with halos atop their heads. God Almighty in his most Beautiful Speech, describes the Angels differently in the Qur'an. From His most Sublime words we know the following:

All praise is due to Allah, Creator of the heavens and the earth, who made the angels messengers having wings, two or three or four. He increases in creation what He wills. Indeed, Allah is over all things competent. -Qur'an 35:1

"They (the Angels) celebrate His praises night and day, nor do they ever slacken." -Quran 21:20

From these two verses, we know that the Angels are, beings with wings. They have one, two, three, or even more wings. In fact, their wings can add up to tens of thousands. They are giant entities that can take the shape of a man when they come down to the Earth.

God Almighty also mentions another fact, and that is that the Angels are neither male nor female. They do not eat, drink, sleep, or reproduce. Unlike human beings they don't need food or water for energy. They never get tired, sick or experience fatigue, they are always in constant motion. They are not like human beings, rather they are an entirely different creation made out of light.

"Those who believe not in the Hereafter name the angels with female names, but they have no knowledge therein. They follow nothing but conjecture, and conjecture avails nothing against Truth". -Quran 53: 27-28

Angels can be feirce and steadfast in obeying the commands of their Lord, these are the Angels for the gates of hell, and even the Angel of Death. Then there are the Angels of Mercy; who bring glad tidings to the messengers, prophets, and righteous people. These Angels come in the shape of extremely clean men, dressed in white. Their clothing is said to be so clean and pure. However, in reality, their original form is something that mankind cannot bear to see. Only the prophets can see the Angels in their natural form and that is only when important message is being conveyed to them, to convey to the people. Human beings cannot bear the sight of Angels, nor will we ever be able to see an Angel in this life.

The Numbers of Angels

There are millions of Angels. Just like there are stars in the universe there are an uncountable number of Angels. Nonetheless, only God Almighty, the sole Creator of all things knows exactly how many Angels there are in the universe.

The place of worship for Muslims is called the masjid. For the Christians, it is called the church, and for the Jewish it is the temples. Angels to have a place of worship that is located in the heavens. The place of worship for the Angels is called; Baytul-Ma'mur or the Frequented House. It is called this because; since the time God created the universe until now, 70,000 Angels went there to worship Almighty God. When a set of 70,000 Angels go there, they never return again. Then another 70,000 come and worship God in the Frequented House, and never return again. Amazing.

Life of Angels

Angels live and breathe to worship God and obey his commands and unlike human beings they do not tire. They are content with repeating the hyms of glorifying Almighty God. They are constantly prostrating their entire being down to the Creator of the heavens and the earth. Angels live to obey God.

Angelic Abilities

Angels have many amazing abilities. They travel faster than the speed of light, they are indescribably strong and are even capable of turning over entire cities like Angel Gabriel did to the towns Sodom and Gomorrah; the people of Lut (Lot). All in all, of these abilities that the Angels have are from the Power and Might of Allah.

Tasks of the Angels

Angels have various duties, with each having a well-defined role. *God Almighty says:*

> **"And there is not any among us, except that has a known position. And we are indeed the ones who glorify Allah." –Qur'an 37:164-166**

The angels possess great powers given to them by God. They can take on different forms. The Qur'an describes how at the moment of Jesus' conception, God sent Gabriel to Mary in the form of a man:

> **"...Then We sent to her Our angel, and he appeared before her as a man in all respects." (Quran 19:17)**

Angels also visited Abraham in human form. Similarly, angels came to Lot to deliver him from danger in the form of handsome, young men. Gabriel used to visit Prophet Muhammad in different forms. Sometimes, he would appear in the form of one of his handsome disciples, and sometimes in the form of a desert Bedouin.

Angels have the ability to take human forms in some circumstances involving common people. As we learn from above, the angels are a grandiose creation of God, varying in numbers, roles, and abilities. God is in no need of these creatures, but having knowledge and belief in them adds to the awe that one feels towards God, in that He is able to create as He wishes, for indeed the magnificence of His creation is a proof of the magnificence of the Creator.

"None knows the hosts of your Lord except Him. It is nothing but a reminder to all human beings." -Quran 74:31

Speed of Light and Angels in the Quran

Angels are low density creatures, Allah created them originally from light. They move at any speed from zero up to the speed of light. It is the angels who carry out God's orders. Those angels take their orders from a Preserved Tablet somewhere in outer space, and not from God's Throne. They commute to and from this Preserved Tablet to get their orders from Allāh. In the following verse, the Quran describes how angels travel when they commute to and from this Tablet. And the speed at which they commute to and from this Tablet turned out to be the known speed of light:

[Quran 32.5] (Allah) Rules the cosmic affair from the heavens to the Earth. Then this affair travels to Him a distance in one day, at a measure of one thousand years of what you count.

It is the angels who carry out these orders. People back then measured the distances neither in kilometers nor in miles but rather by how much time they needed to walk. For example, a village two days away meant a distance equivalent to walking for two days; ten days away meant a distance equivalent to walking for ten days. However, in this verse the Quran specifies 1000 years of what they counted (not what they walked). They also followed the lunar calendar and counted 12 lunar months each year. These months are related to the moon and not related to the sun.

Hence in 1 day the angels will travel a distance of 1000 years of what they counted (the moon). Since this verse is referring to distance, then God is saying that angels travel in one day the same distance that the moon travels in 12000 lunar orbits. 12000 Lunar Orbits/Earth Day = distance/time = rate of motion (speed). However, this speed depends on the frame of reference, that is, you could define million different frames and get million different results. But if you want to compare it with the speed of light in local inertial frames then you need to make the comparison in a local inertial frame.

The month for the Arabs was 29.5 Earth days, but Earth (the reference frame) was and still is non-inertial. 299792.458 km/sec is the measured speed of light in local inertial frames. These are different frames. To overcome this discrepancy in frames we are calculating 12000 Lunar Orbits/Earth Day when the geocentric frame is inertial and then comparing it with 299792.458 km/sec. This is in essence the speed at which light travels.

The Authenticity of the Quran

Unlike other scriptures worldwide, the Quran is the only widely copied book that is kept in its original language. Of course, there are translations of the Qur'an in many different languages, however we main language it is recited in is Arabic. The language it is read, memorized and studied in is in Arabic. The reason for this is because as Muslims we strive to keep the authentic version of the Qur'an. We strive to keep it pure from any altercations, changes, or other versions. In fact, people who are non-Arabic speakers, like myself, also read the Quran fluently in its original language.

From personal experience, I know of people who converted to Islam and can fluently read the Quran in Arabic. This causes Muslims to stay in touch with the original composition of the Quran. God states in the Quran in numerous verses that He has made the Quran easier to remember and to memorize. One of the reasons why I truly believe in Islam, is because of that fact that millions of Muslims from every background and all around the world, have memorized the Quran. It is the most memorized book in the universe! This means, that if all copies of every scripture from every religion were to be thrown out into the ocean, and the Qur'an was among the scriptures.

The Qur'an would be the only book in the entire world that can be reproduced within a few days.
This shows that when God said he has promised to protect the Qur'an from human corruption, He the Almighty is speaking the truth!

The fact that God (in the Qur'an) has given credibility to the two former Abrahamic religions; Christianity and Judaism shows that Islam was not sent to repel the two religions. Rather it was sent as a verification and a correction to the books that were sent to messengers aforetime.

O ye who believe! Believe in Allah and His Apostle, and the scripture which He hath sent to His Apostle and the scripture which He sent to those before (him). Any who denies Allah, His Angels, His Books, His Apostles, and the Day of Judgement, hath gone far, far astray (Qur'an 4:136).
And those who say...we believe in Allah, and in what has been revealed to us and what was revealed to Abraham, Ismail, Isaac, Jacob, and the Tribes, and in (the Books) given to Moses, Jesus, and the Prophets, from their Lord: We make no distinction between one and another among them (Qur'an 3:84).

How come they (come) unto thee (Muhammad) for judgment when they have the Torah, wherein Allah hath delivered judgment (for them)? ... Lo! We did reveal the Torah, wherein is guidance and a light ... And We caused Jesus, son of Mary, to follow in their footsteps, confirming that which was (revealed) before him in the Torah, and We bestowed on him the Gospel wherein is guidance and a light, confirming that which was (revealed) before it in the Torah – a guidance and an admonition unto those who ward off (evil). Let the People of the Gospel judge by that which Allah hath revealed therein. Whoso judges not by that which Allah hath revealed: such are evil-livers.

And unto thee (Muslims) have We revealed the Scripture (the Qur'an) with the truth, confirming whatever Scripture was before it, and a watcher over it. So, judge between them by that which Allah hath revealed, and follow not their desires away from the truth which hath come unto thee. **For each We have appointed a divine law and a traced-out way. Had Allah willed He could have made you one community. But that He may try you by that which He hath given you (He hath made you as ye are).** *So, vie one with another in good works. Unto Allah ye will all return, and He will then inform you of that wherein ye differ. (5:43-48)*

We reveal to you as We revealed to Noah, and the prophets after him, and as We inspired Abraham and Ishmael and Isaac and Jacob and the tribes, and Jesus, Job and Jonah, Aaron and Solomon, and as we imparted the Psalms unto David. Messengers, We have mentioned unto you before, and Messengers We have not mentioned to you. And God spoke unto Moses directly. (4:163-64)

The fact that the Qur'an has ONE central theme is enough for me to believe in it.
Main central theme: Your Lord, God, (Allah), is ONE. He sent prophets to guide mankind.

Those prophets were sent with a warning, and good news. They were also sent with miracles.
Each messenger that was sent with a message had one mission. Their mission was to convey to the people that there is One God.

The good news that they conveyed to the people was that if they obeyed they would meet their Creator and enter eternal bliss in heaven. The warning was that if they witnessed the truth, their miracles, and still refused they would be among those that God will punish.

Islam is that simple. There are no loops, there are no other characters, there is no confusion in its message, therefore there is no other way. Islam wasn't sent exclusively to one group of people, it wasn't sent for preachers, teachers, sheikhs and Imams to study. It was sent for all of mankind.
That alone shows that the Qur'an is inclusive to all of creation and not just to a certain few.
The Qur'an is a book of wisdom and knowledge. It's a book that conveys to its reader the very essence of a perfect society. It contains elements of proper governance to an entire nation to how individuals should conduct their personal lives. It's a book of advice, and is factually proven to be able to change a person into a better human being for himself and for others around him. It's a book of history, a book that contains true aspects of how the world around us runs. Most

of all the Qur'an is a book of truth. Every single verse in the Qur'an can be backed up by real and evident explanation.

The Quran stresses the importance of good character and good conduct. Nowhere in Gods speech is there an interference with evil, wrongdoing, or misconduct. This in itself, is proof that those who don't know about the Qur'an are missing out on the greatest treasure ever known to mankind.

God is Neither Feminine nor Masculine

Allah the most High is not like us, and doesn't look like us. God is no need of food and water. Neither slumber nor sleep overtakes Him. He does not need any of His creation, rather we need Him. The name 'Allah' is a universal name of God. It is the actual name of God. One of significance about the name 'Allah' is the fact that it cannot be neither masculine nor feminine. Unlike, 'god' which can be come 'gods' for more gods, and 'goddesses' for woman gods; the name 'Allah' cannot be transformed. It is a fixed name and doesn't change grammatically to mean something else. Then there comes the fact that the language God chose for the Qur'an *'Arabic'*; does not contain the word *'it'*.

In Arabic, there are only two parts; and they are the two genders, male and female. Every single thing that is named in Arabic is divided into a 'male category' or a 'female category'.
For example: "Al-Qamar" (Moon), is a masculine word and "Al-Shams" (Sun), is a feminine word.

Whether the word is an inanimate object or not, they are put into a male category or a female category; no such thing as IT.

The male category is two categories.

Masculine Haqeeqi (Real): This is used for masculine genders for humans and animals.
Masculine Majezi (Unreal): This is when it is used as masculine but in reality, it is not. These have their own categories but are referred to has masculine. Inanimate objects, the moon, a pen, Angels (Malak), Night (Layl), and even Door (baab). The divine name of Allah falls into this category. This does mean that Allah is unreal. This means that Allahs name is used this way grammatically in the Arabic language.

Allah is unique and cannot be referred as 'it' in English, since Allah has no gender, neither male nor female, rather the name is in the neutral category. *Some people may argue that the Arabic word 'huwa' (He) and 'hiya' (She) both can be used for 'it' or neutral gender, then why Allah has used 'huwa' (He) and not 'hiya' (She)?*

In Arabic grammar, there are certain rules and criteria for feminine gender. First, if it is female by nature, like the word mother (ummum), it becomes feminine in gender. Allah is not a female. Second, if it ends with the third Arabic letter 'ta' like 'mirwahtun' (fan), it becomes feminine. The Arabic word 'Allah' doesn't end with 'ta' so it cannot be feminine. Third, if the word ends with 'Alif Mamduda' (big Alif), it becomes feminine. But the Arabic word 'Allah' doesn't end with 'Alif Mamduda' so, it cannot be feminine. And lastly, if the object occurs in pairs, like pairs of the body, e.g. 'Ainun' (eyes), 'yadun' (hands), they are considered feminine. Reference: IslamVoice

So the part of God referring to Himself has He in the Qur'an does not mean he is a physically masculine. These rulings clearly explain that God referring to Himself as He is the grammatically correct way to refer to Himself in the Arabic language. This is why god refers to Himself as "Huwa" or *He* in the Qur'an.

When God Takes an Oath in the Quran

In many verses in the Qur'an God takes an oath. Many of the verses start with, "...and I swear by...", "And I take oath by the...." "And by the..." Looking closely at the background of the Qur'an we understand that it was not revealed to the same people the Bible and the Torah were revealed to. The Bible was revealed to the Jesus (May Gods peace be upon him), his people were the people living in Palestine, among them Armenians, Israelites, Arabs, and even Persians. The Qur'an, however, was revealed to the people of the dessert in Arabia. To be exact in the two locations of Mecca and Medina.

During those times, the Arabians of Mecca used to regularly take Oath on certain topics, especially during important occasions or discussions. When an Arab or any other person who has adapted to the culture of the Arabians in Mecca or Medina would take an oath they would do it for the following reasons:

1) When they want to grab the attention of their audience of the person they are speaking to.
ex: "I hereby take an oath..." This usually used in American courts, when important matters are being discussed or when a defendant is taking an oath that they are completely innocent.

2) When they are about to introduce a very important subject or topic. An example could be taking an oath on becoming an American citizen. A person becoming must show that they will be loyal to the US and the American flag, thus they take an oath in public, so that it will be known that they undertook that promise.

3) When they are speaking of something they love or admire. An example, regarding modern times, would be when a person is talking to their friend and they say, "I swear I just love that jacket.." Now, that being said God took important Oaths in the most amazing Qur'an...

In one particular chapter of the Quran (91:1-7) God says the following:

1) By the sun and its brightness
2) And by the moon when it follows it
3) And by the day when it displays it
4) Ad by the night when it covers it
5) And by the sky and He who constructed it
6) And by the earth and He who spread it
7) And by the soul and He who proportioned it
8) And inspired the soul with either wickedness or righteousness
9) he has succeeded who purifies it
10) and he has failed who instills it with corruption

This chapter is the only chapter in the Qur'an where Allah strikes the readers with a long line of Oaths. Since, taking an Oath at the time meant getting the reader recognize the importance of what was being discussed, these verses are pointing out what God wants you to recognize.

That being said, there is a verse in the Qur'an in which God Almighty states that He has taken the Greatest Oath and it goes as following:

"And I take an Oath by the placement of the star* And it is a great Oath if you only knew* It is the Noble Qur'an*" Surah Waqia

Looking at these verses one may ask, why in the world would God take an Oath by the placement of the star? When in fact every single of His creation knows that the star is placed in the sky?

Recalling earlier I mentioned the reason to taking an Oath due to the environment the Qur'an was sent in. Well, here God is calling our attention to an important topic, and that is. In order to see the placement of the star one must be a traveler. Since stars can't be seen during the day, this traveler must be one traveling in the night. So, this means this traveler is essentially enveloped in darkness. The only positive influences the traveler has are the stars, because stars were created as a means of guidance for travelers. That being said, God mentions that this is indeed a great Oath and following that he mentions the Noble Qur'an.

When you look at it this way, one will understand that as humans we are traveler's leaving this world and traveling to the next. Just like that traveler looking for guidance in the stars, we are in need of guidance.

That guidance for us is the most Noble Qur'an and Allah is the Most Knowledgeable and All-Aware of all that we say or do.

The Unseen and the Mysterious: The Jinn

After countless hours of research and studying what the Quran and ahadith (teachings of the Prophet Muhammad), state about the jinn, this is the following that I have gathered:

In order for you to get the whole picture about the Jinn I will have to first take you through some history and characteristics then explain several phenomena around the world related to the Jinn.

THE JINN

The word Jinn (Djinn) is an Arabic word meaning "to hide" or "hidden".

The Jinn are hidden from our sight and are considered to be spiritual beings similar to angels.

The Jinn are mentioned mainly in Islam but also have some links to Christianity, regarding Prophet Solomon.

Jinnī (Genie), is the singular form of Jinn.

According to a translation of the Quran by Mufti Taqi Usmani, the father of the Jinn is called Jānn, just as the father of mankind is Adam.

Jann was said to be created from a substance that was as blazing as fire, but subtle as wind.

"from a fire of scorching wind" [Quran 15:27]

"from a smokeless flame of fire" [Quran 55:15]

The Jinn are mentioned in the Quran in approximately 28 instances. Therefore, the earliest book that talks about the Jinn would be the Quran (1400 years old). Jinn stories can be found in the book called 'One Thousand and One Nights', which is a collection folk tales compiled in Arabic. The English version is known as the Arabian Nights.

SOME HISTORY

Suleimān (King Solomon—son of David) was a prophet of ancient Israel. He was bestowed upon with special powers or gifts by God which include wisdom in his youth, talking to birds and having control over the Jinn. He was also known to be a great preacher.

In the Quran, Prophet Suleiman talks to the Jinn and people, to bring the throne of the Queen of Saba' (Sheba – some say Sheba is Yemen).

Chapter 27 Verses 38-40 Translation: Yusuf Ali

Said an Ifrit of the Jinns: "I will bring it to thee before thou rise from thy Council: indeed I have full strength for the purpose, and may be trusted." (39)

the main thing to be noted here is the travelling speed of the jinni.

According to the Quran, humans and Jinn will both face the day of Judgement and be punished or rewarded according to their deeds (i.e. both have free will).

A Jinnī called Iblis used his free will and refused to bow to Adam and was therefore expelled from the heavens and was declared Shaytān (Satan) meaning "the opposer" and in the Quran Allah says, "He is of the Jinn". The throne of Iblis is said to be over water.

It is still not clearly understood whether Jinn are angels or Jinn are a tribe of angels or a separate entity altogether, but I will leave that for the scholars to decide.

Fortune telling was a common practice before /during and after the time of the prophet Muhammad. The fortune tellers before the time of the Prophet Muhammad were very accurate. The reason for the fortune teller's great accuracy was that the gates to the heavens were open to the jinn. The jinn used to listen to the commands of the Almighty and relay the message to the fortune teller. During the time of the Prophet Muhammad, new barriers were placed with guards to distance the Jinn from the truth and therefore the accuracy in fortune telling went downhill.

Every human is believed to have one angel and one jinni with them at all times. The angel is there to note everything you do and writes down all your deeds in a book attached to your neck, as well as report your daily and nightly deeds to God. The jinni is there to lead you astray. when a person dies the jinni is relieved of it's duty and is free to roam the earth to cause more mischief, until the jinni dies. The lifespan of the jinni is not known clearly. Some say they live for 1000 years, others say up to 8000 years.

TYPES OF JINN

Some people believe there are tribes and not types of Jinn. I found more logical sense in the types rather than tribes during my research, therefore will stick to the types of Jinn in this hub.

There are 4 types of Jinn:

Sílā

Ghūl
Ifrīt
Mārid
Note: If there had to be only one type of Jinn out of these four then it would be the Ifrīt. There could also be Ranks among the Jinn instead of types. The Ifrīt are mentioned in some Quran translations and the Hadith

The Sila:

The sílā are believed to be female. They are a rare, and It is not known which areas they inhabit on earth. They are reserved and secretive. They have a sense of being very independent. They are excellent shape shifters. They also can manipulate circumstances around you but is only an illusion which makes them great in the art of manipulating others for a short time. They are believed to be the most intelligent of the jinn. They can become a human's companion. Some people confuse the sílā with the Ghūl because it is difficult to differentiate between them.

[Source: Non-Muslim Forum – see reference links at end of article]

The Ghūl:

The Ghūl are believed to be female, that inhabit burial grounds and other deserted places. They are evil jinn and are said to be the offspring of Iblīs (Shaytān). They are also shape shifters but can be recognized by their unchangeable sign; the ass's hooves.

"A ghūl stalked the desert, often in the guise of an attractive woman, trying to distract travelers, and, when successful, killed and ate them. The sole defense that one had against a ghūl was to strike it dead in one blow; a second blow would only bring it back to life again."

[Source: Britannica encyclopedia online]

One thing to note here is that the throne of Iblis is in the waters yet the offspring (Ghul) inhabit burial grounds and deserted places. The throne part is from the Hadith which are more reliable than the internet so if any of the two statements are wrong it would be the ghul inhabiting burial grounds and deserted places.

The Ifreet

Ifrīt means "rebellious". They can be male (Ifrīt) or female (Ifrītah). Like humans they have good and bad ones between them but are depicted as being wicked and ruthless. They inhabit the underground and ruins. Ifrīts have a whole structured society complete with kings, tribes and clans. They are known to have enormous wings and look like they are made out of smoke. They are susceptible to magic, which humans can use to kill or capture and enslave them. An Ifrīt can be a believer or unbeliever, and have the same belief system as humans (i.e. Jews, Christians, Muslim, Atheist, Sikh, Hindu, and Buddhist). It is difficult to differentiate between an Ifrīt and a Mārid as they have very similar characteristics.

[Source: Britannica encyclopedia online]

Marid:

Mārid are described to be the most powerful type of jinn having great powers and inhabit the oceans, seas and open waters. They are the most arrogant and proud of all the jinn types. They do grant wishes to humans but it requires some kind of battle, rituals, imprisonment or even a great deal of flattery.

[Source: Britannica encyclopedia online]

Note – I would have assumed the Marid to be the offsprings of Iblis (Saytan) as they inhabit similar regions as well as being the most powerful.

References:

The term Hadīth (plural: hadīth, or ahadīth) in Islām is a body of Authentic literature that comprises the sayings, teachings, behaviour and characteristics of the last messenger of God; Prophet Muhammad. The Hadīth is a key source of information for Muslims, who try to emulate the character and apply the teachings of the Prophet Muhammad in their everyday lives.

There are over 50 hadith which talk about the Jinn and I would like to share 3 with you.

Bukhari: Book 1 :: Volume 8 :: Hadith 450

Narrated Abu Huraira:

"The Prophet said, "Last night a big demon (afreet) from the Jinns came to me and wanted to interrupt my prayers (or said something similar) but Allah enabled me to overpower him. I wanted to fasten him to one of the pillars of the mosque so that all of you could See him in the morning but I remembered the statement of my brother Solomon (as stated in Quran): My Lord! Forgive me and bestow on me a kingdom such as shall not belong to anybody after me (38.35)." The sub narrator Rauh said, "He (the demon) was dismissed humiliated."

Notes

afreet is a different spelling of Ifrīt

Aisha was the wife of Prophet Muhammad

Abu Huraira and Jabir bin 'Abdullah were companions of Prophet
Muhammad.

Bukhari: Book 4 :: Volume 54 :: Hadith 533

Narrated Jabir bin 'Abdullah:

The Prophet said, "Cover your utensils and tie your water skins, and
close your doors and keep your children close to you at night, as the
Jinns spread out at such time and snatch things away. When you go to
bed, put out your lights, for the mischief-doer (i.e. the rat) may drag
away the wick of the candle and burn the dwellers of the house." Ata
said, "The devils." (instead of the Jinns).

Bukhari:: Book 7 :: Volume 71 :: Hadith 657

Narrated 'Aisha:

Some people asked Allah's Apostle about the fore-tellers He said. 'They are nothing" They said, 'O Allah's Apostle! Sometimes they tell us of a thing which turns out to be true." Allah's Apostle said, "A Jinn snatches that true word and pours it into the ear of his friend (the fore-teller) (as one puts something into a bottle) The foreteller then mixes with that word one hundred lies."

CAN THEY BE ENSLAVED OR CAPTURED?

The straight forward answer is yes they can. On some certain non-Muslims forums I've read about people even creating a family of Jinn and spirits for themselves and being light, dark and grey. One important aspect to remember is if the Jinn have free will like humans then they will not always be telling the truth. If they are evil jinn then they will become whatever you want them to be to drive you astray.

The Islamic scholars say they are the unseen and cannot be seen yet many non-Muslims claim they have seen them. One possibility could be that they cannot be seen in their actual state but can be seen if they modify their state.

In order to capture them you need to have a vessel of some kind with a precious stone in it which is liked by the jinn, where they can live with you and there is some kind of welcoming ritual involved where you raise the vessel in a tea light and introduce yourself to them and welcome them as well as ask them to protect and guide you and to stay with you in the vessel till you die, and some other wordings are involved to start creating a bond between the human and the jinn.

In other cases, you do not welcome them but you must have an article that belongs to that particular jinni. If the jinni is unwilling to be bound then the person and the jinn engage in a batter of mind games/riddles in order to obtain the others true name. The games are said to be long and dangerous and the winner can choose to enslave or kill the other.

For believers in God – It is not advisable to take this route as in some cases you have to start calling them your Protector, and are asking for guidance. Only God is the Protector and the one who provides Guidance. I believe this is a trap for the believer as they start associating something else with God.

PHENOMENA ASSOCIATED WITH THE JINN
Visions of dead people

Because everyone has a jinni attached to them in this world, when the person dies their jinni is released. This jinni knows the shape of your close relative who has passed away. The jinni can come in the shape of your family member and talk to you. There could be good intentions of the jinni as well as bad. For some people it helps get over the sorrow of losing a loved one, knowing they are well and safe. Since the jinni has lived with the relative all their lives the jinni will know everything about the person and can speak about memories and everything.

Shadow people

Jinni's can form the shape of a shadow and stand on top of you or on the side of your bed. It just stands and watches people. I have no idea why it stares at the person and even lets them see that someone is watching them, but I will assume that they might want their presence to be recognized by the specific person who sees the jinni. The reason I say a specific person is because it has happened to a friend of mine who saw the shadow standing on top of him but when he woke his family member up to show her, she could not see anything.

Sleep paralysis

I've been through sleep paralysis and I know it feels like someone is grabbing hold of you and you cannot move at all. I believe it's a jinni who might either be obsessed with you and is giving you a hug, or a jinni who is angry with you, who might want you out of the house or the way and giving you a warning. Your bed could be in the jinni's everyday path and since you're blocking the route the jinni gets frustrated and makes sure you know something you've done is wrong. Some might just do it for the fun of scaring the daylights out of the person.

Appear in the form of saints

There are a number of stories where people see a pious person or a saint who says to the person in their dream that all your sins are forgiven and you no longer need to pray. People do fall for these kinds of dreams or visions and quit their prayers. It's obviously a bad jinni doing a good job in the eyes of Satan.

Fortune Tellers

They will look at you for a second or two and then tell you something correct and secretive about your past. How does that work? The fortune teller has an enslaved jinni, he then makes the jinni ask your jinni about your life and the information is relayed to the fortune teller. This is how they know things about you. Once they have built your trust that they know what no one knows, then they start telling you false information about your future.

Black magic

Powerful jinn are used in black magic, probably the Mārid. It is believed that there is some sort of contract between the jinn and the practitioner of black magic. Contracts could include sacrifice of animals or even a disrespectful act such as urinating on religious scriptures. These jinn are sent by the practitioner to possess you. They cause aches and pains as well as diseases which cannot be diagnosed by doctors. If the black magic is strong enough then it can even take your life. Black magic also causes stoppages in ones daily errands and makes the affected person's life really difficult. Some people would not be able to get married no matter how hard they try, at the end of the day something goes wrong. Some people might suffer financially. Some people would have to try a couple of times to get a single task completed. All these are variations in black magic. In black magic as far as I've heard, people are used as vessels for travel. I have no idea how it works and why a black magician would need a vessel but the person performing black magic would be using the jinn. I also know that some UFO aircraft seen have been military undercover projects, and for some reason if there is a large object in the sky the governments never attack it for being in their air space.

Aliens and Abductions

Once again the Jinn. I recently saw a true story movie called "the fourth kind", where people were being abducted in Nome, Alaska. The lady in the movie saw black shadows who had dragged her out of bed while she was asleep and maybe did an experiment or two on her, but she never remembered anything until she heard a recording. The beings were possessing people in Nome and also claimed that it was God. The possessed people were either severely injured or killed after the message of the being had been relayed. The original footages are also shown in the movie but whenever the jinn arrived or wanted to show themselves the visual recording and audio became scrambled.

Magicians

Similar to black magic we have magicians who use the jinn to entertain people. I know most magicians are actually very good illusionists, but some who do great stunts in front of a 3D crowd have some jinn under their sleeves.

Psychics

Psychics I've only seen in the west. There is nothing like it in the east or I have not personally come across a psychic in the east. I do not know how much in depth information a psychic can reveal about the dead person but if they are only things that match the person they are working for then they are not in touch with the dead but the jinni of the person sitting in front of them. They can get all the information from the jinni inside you if you go to the psychic. They just don't know who's jinni is talking to them but I do believe they have the ability to communicate to the jinn.

Ghosts & Hauntings

Spirits of dead people do not leave the graves. The people in the grave are asleep and will wake up on the day of judgement feeling like they have slept for something like 10 days. As we know the Jinn occupy empty places, this tells me there could be a family of jinn living in the haunted house, and do not want people to move in because the house is occupied. The easiest way is to frighten the people who visit to secure the location.

Ouija board

Almost all the people interested in the paranormal have tried the Ouija board. In my view you are not talking to a dead person you are talking to any jinn that is present in your house at the time. Yes they do have names. They cannot tell you the correct future. They might be able to tell you about your past while talking to the jinn attached to you.

Spontaneous Combustion

I might be stretching it out a little, but it's a thought that came across my mind. It could be possible that this phenomenon can be related to the Jinn as well. As discussed earlier the human has to battle with the jinn in order to capture or enslave a jinn. If the human loses the battle maybe the jinn burns him with the fire he/she was created with. Maybe the human was mistreating the jinn and the jinn wanted revenge and killed him/her. Could be a possibility. I have personally never come across anyone who knew a person who passed away this way therefore i cannot verify if they were in any contact with beings before their death.

Bermuda Triangle

We know the throne of Iblis (Saytan) is over water. It could be possible that the Bermuda triangle is where the throne of Iblis is situated. People who make it out alive, see all kinds of illusions in the Bermuda Triangle and it could be the jinn creating the illusions. We also know electronic devices fail in the Bermuda Triangle and we also know that when the jinn want their presence known the electronic devices do not function well. There could be a link but once again only a guess.

Pyramids of Egypt

This is also another possibility not a fact. We know the pyramids have a link to astrology, where the tunnels point towards a specific point in the sky. We also know people worshipped the jinn in the past, and we also know the jinn have great strengths. Jinn also have a link to teaching magic and fortune telling man therefore i think it is quite safe to assume that there is a possibility that the jinn were the gods of the people of the time and they constructed the pyramids.

PROTECTION FROM JINN AND BLACK MAGIC

There are many ways to protect yourself from a Jinn but most of them are Islamic methods which i will write about in a different hub.

One thing I can share here for readers of all faiths is to dispose your nails and hair properly. Also guard your mother's name, meaning do not tell people your mother's name. If someone wants magic done on you they will need one or all of these items.

Most spiritual healing type people I have personally visited have asked for the following.

a picture of the person.
the address of the person
the mothers name of the person
If the healers can use this information to get to a person who lives over 7,000 miles away within seconds, then this information can be equally dangerous if it falls in the wrong hands. One possibility can be the healer is an expert astral traveler and using their power of travel to misguide you.

Another thing we know is that the devil or jinns spread out just after sunset. So to make sure they do not stay over in an abandoned room in your house, you should to switch on a light in every room when the sun is about to set and leave the light on for 30 mins or so.

A strong warning for my brothers and sisters in Islam. If you go to a spiritual healing person and they ask for names and pictures then please do not supply the information and walk out. Moving forward with this kind of healing is not the right way in Islam, and many scholars have declared that as soon as you provide that information, to the healer you have stepped out of the boundaries of Islam. The correct way is to perform Ruqya. You can do it yourself or get a knowledgeable person to perform Ruqya on the possessed or affected person. (More in another Hub, you can search google for Ruqya and you'll get many results)

Muslim:: Book 1 : Hadith 343

Abu Musa reported: The Messenger of Allah (may peace be upon him) was standing amongst us and he told us five things. He said: Verily the Exalted and Mighty God does not sleep, and it does not befit Him to sleep. He lowers the scale and lifts it. The deeds in the night are taken up to Him before the deeds of the day. and the deeds of the day before the deeds of the night. His veil is the light. In the hadith narrated by Abu Bakr (instead of the word" light") it is fire. If he withdraws it (the veil), the splendor of His countenance would consume His creation so far as His sight reaches.

FINALLY…

And there we have it, from ghosts, shape shifters, man eaters, illusionists to flying around the world and even up to the heavens and back within seconds. The Jinn are truly powerful beings that live parallel to us in this world.

I would like to leave you with the thought that if we have such enormous beings which are capable of so much in this world then how Great, Powerful and Enormous would the Creator, the Almighty be…
Is there anything unseen to the Jinn?

Quran Surah 34:14

"King Solomon had entrusted the construction of Bait-ul-Maqdis (Jerusalem) to the Jinns. They used to work only under the supervision of Solomon. When the time of his death approached, he stood before them (in his place of worship) reclining on his scepter. When he died in this position, his body remained standing with the support of the scepter. The Jinns, believing him to be alive, continued their work until the remaining work was completed. At that point Allah sent a termite that ate up the wood of the scepter, and the body of Solomon fell down. Then the Jinns came to know about his death. This incident also falsified the presumption that the Jinns have the knowledge of the Unseen." Quran Commentary: Mufti Taqi Usmani.

Part 3: More Insight and Wisdom

The Remembrance of Allah

"Verily, by the Remembrance of Allah do hearts find peace." Qur'an 13:28

Islam is an endlessly deep and vast pool of knowledge. It is impossible to ever explain the beauty of Islam in its entirety but I will hit upon important points; that will direct you to its beauty.

The above verse explains the affect Remembering God has on humans. It gives us a peace and tranquility that we can find nowhere else in this world. It is such an amazing feeling, and once that extraordinary feeling is achieved; a feeling of surety is created.

"Since the heart is the central organ of a human being, the effect of a tranquil, peaceful heart has a profound effect on the body and mind of a human being. This leads to the second main benefit and objective of the practice, namely, to move away from bad habits and character traits, in order to manifest that peace and balance experienced by the heart in all areas of one's life." Beautiful insight from the website beauty of Islam.

When God is remembered constantly a person is aware of Him, therefore a person will be more cautious of what he or she does. They will make sure every action they do will be ultimately pleasing to their Lord. This is why a person feels peace, contentment and serenity in their hearts because they will be more devoted to what is the most important in the whole entire universe, and that is God. In return, a person will feel more important, they will feel that they have a sense of purpose and a drive to lead an excellent life.

153

Islam is widely misinterpreted and criticized. Many of the prophets in history were criticized and many of the prophets were also mocked. Even people of truth, and the noble prophets went through hardships, tribulations, and were mocked, taunted and ridiculed by their own people and even others. Islam teaches every individual to not expect the love of others, but the Love of Allah. And that if many among the creation of Allah do not love Him, then what do we expect if we try to be loved by everyone? We will ultimately fail. Because, the lifestyle an individual chooses to live should not be chosen based upon the love of people. Once this is done, then a person no longer lives for themselves, for their own benefit but the benefit of others. And this is what can lead to a person's own downfall and loss. The greatest benefit in the heart of man is to remember Allah constantly.

Because it is only through his remembrance that peace can be attained. And true mindfulness of Allah can only happen if one lives according to the way the Creator has ordained. This means to follow the way of Allah whether those around you love it or not. And this is what leads to true freedom from the shackles of society. Once you follow your Creator above the ideals of any society in this passing world; the path to true peace and serenity will be paved for you and you will be welcome to the gates to His mercy and love.

You have 3 Brains: The Head, The Gut, The Heart

The Head: the seat of logic and intellect, however, the unconscious mind directs around 90% of our behaviors.

The Gut: 90% of the body's serotonin, involved in mood and management, is produced in the gut, eat well to feel well.

The Heart: There are more neural pathways running from the heart to the head brain than from the head brain to the heart.

The heart is described as the source of intellect in the Quran. Is it really think before you speak, or feel before you do? What you feel is what you say, usually. Qalb ( ), or heart, is the origin of intentional activities, the cause behind all human intuitive deeds. The brain handles the physical impressions, but the qalb (the heart) is responsible for apprehending.

As conscious beings, we have a feeling that our consciousness or mind is somewhere in the region of our heart. This has been the feeling of humans from the very beginning, and we use expressions like: "I speak from the bottom of my heart," "a heart to hear talk," "heart has its reasons, which reason does not know," etc.

Allah says in the Quran: "Will they not, then, reflect over the Quran? Or are there locks upon their hearts?" 47:24. The Quran notes the deepest of reflections happens in the heart. Some people's hearts are locked in this world and so is their ability to truly see this illusion that we are living in for what it is.

One researcher said, "we observed the heart was acting as though it has a mind of its own and was profoundly affecting perception, intelligence, and awareness." It is also noteworthy that recent research in the relevant fields show that our heart even contains thousands of specialized neurons similar to those in the brain, and the brain and the heart work in close connection. Neurons are what allow our brain to form thoughts. While much about the neurons in our heart is still unknown, one thing is for sure – the 'brain' in our heart communicates back and forth with the brain in the head. It's a two-way street.

In conclusion, the heart senses emotional information five to seven seconds before it happens, while the brain senses it three to five seconds beforehand. So not only are emotions important contributors to the output of our thoughts, but they may be one of the best wats to influence and create a change in what and how we think. Again, "do they not have hearts with which to reason?" Quran 22:46

Some Wisdom about the Heart and Love

Loving yourself, is loving Allah – loving yourself is just as vital when it comes to faith. When you love your being, you are in return being grateful to Allah for all the favors you've been given. The body is as ephemeral as this world, as viable as a candle – it is brief and temporary. There might be a voice in your head, a moment of self-doubt where you feel you are not deserving of life and the eternity promised, but you are wrong. Allah assures us in the Quran, that humans are the best of creation. That our body has been created in the most excellent of form. That our conscious is from an eternal spirit that Allah has blown into us, that will live on for eternity.

It only makes sense to take care of this gift, mentally, emotionally and spiritually. To regard our time as sacred, and our space as sacred by choosing carefully who we allow into it. This won't prove to be an easy journey, because within the arena of your heart there are battles between the factions of love and hate; intolerance and benevolence, self-assurance, and self-doubt, but I think this is why the reward is so great in the end. The ones who overcome will be rewarded with virtues that are the keys to entering paradise.

Lastly, keep in mind that your soul is greater than this world and everything that is in it. The number goal of Iblees, is to increase in your eyes, the value of temporal things, and take away the insight you have about yourself and your self-power – all of that is within you.

Every messenger of God from Jesus to Moses and David, all taught one thing – to keep the world in one hand, but also hold to your connection with God in the other. Balance is key. Your power isn't through your money (looks), body, or this temporary world. It lies in your spirit; the key is to make sure we aren't distracted and forget this. In return, this self-knowledge will raise you in status (in the heavens and maybe on earth), and gift you with serenity.

Remember, peaceful is the one who is not concerned with having more or less, unbound by name and fame, that nafs (spirit) is free from sorrow, the world, and mostly itself. Bet on yourself, invest in your "self" and "spirit", you are your most important asset.

Signs of a Spiritual Awakening

Are you having a spiritual awakening? These are some signs that you just elevated in your mindset, and in your spirit:

-   You desire to be alone, you crave solitude; whereas once you may have been extroverted, now you experience and appreciate the introverted side of your nature. You spend more time introspecting and enjoying silence. You try to reduce social contact a little more, spend your time more wisely, and find more value in your alone time.

-   Conversations seem shallow, when you talk to people you feel an acute sense of separation. You realize that very few people are capable of talking about passion, emotions, meaning, and the soul. In conversations, you feel restless and irritated by too much talk, and small talk.

-   You thirst for authenticity and truth, and being true to yourself becomes top priority. You hate faking and putting on old masks that you used to wear. You want to be completely authentic.

Pretense makes you feel sick and disgusted. You also admire authentic and meaningful relations, you view them as gems for your journey in life.

- You become aware of your old negative habits. You are painfully aware of your flaws and destructive habits. You are also aware of your good habits and seek to cultivate them more. Consistency becomes an aspiration for you. Within you arises a strong urge to wipe the slate clean and start over.

- You experience anxiety and/or depression. You may go through deep bouts of existential depression and/or deep anxiety. The shock of plunging into your awakening leaves you feeling unstable. You may be misdiagnosed with a mental illness. Uncertainty and fear of the future follow you everywhere.

These are some of the emotions you will go through as you continue to grow and elevate spiritually in life, and remember growth is pain – it is not comfortable, and isn't meant to be. However, once you weather the storm and go through it, you will come out a wise spirit and have so much lessons and beautiful wisdom to share with your loved ones now and in the future.

What is the Difference Between a Prophet (Nabi) and Messenger (Rasul)

Every messenger is a Prophet, but not every Prophet is a Messenger. A messenger receives a message (divine revelation) and conveys it to their people. A Prophet receives revelations mostly in the form of dreams but is not obligated to convey it to the world. Instead, Prophets conveyed the message to those closest to them; like family members or their specific villages or communities. Prophet Muhamad said there were over 124,000 prophets who guided people to God (Allah), only a few were mentioned in the Quran.

Examples of Prophets are: prophet Adam, the father of humankind. He conveyed the message to his children. Prophet Yusuf (Joseph). He conveyed the message to prisoner of Egypt when he was unjustly confined. Prophet Harun (Aaron), he willingly worked alongside his brother Messenger Moses (who received the Torah) to help convey the message to the Children of Israel.

According to authentic narrations one of the key differences between a prophet and messenger is whether they could see and visit the angel of revelation.

According to those narrations a prophet is one who can see Angel Gabriel in their dream, hear him but cannot see him when he is awake. A messenger can see the angel in their dream, and when they are awake as well. As a recap: a prophet just conveys the message, a messenger gets a book of revelation and actively teaches it until the mission is complete.

Manu times Prophet was mentored by their father who was a messenger. Example: Abraham (peace be upon him) is a messenger and a prophet. He traveled to convey the message to the world. His children Isaak and Ismael were just prophets, but learned from him.

References from the Quran on the above:

There were many prophets who just conveyed truth without a specific mission:

1. "And We sent many prophets to you, there are some We have mentioned to you and others we have not mentioned..." Quran 40:78

Messengers; with miracles, books, a warning, and a mission:

2. And we sent messengers, as bringers of good tidings and warned so
that mankind will have no argument against Allah after the messengers.
And ever is Allah Exalted in Might and Wise." Quran 41:65

Proof that Prophets and Messengers were Sent by God

If anyone came to you right now and told you that they have a message
from God and that he is a messenger, you would think he is a lunatic,
right? If they told you; hey come on Samantha, you got to believe in
me, I am a man sent from God! You would probably run away. All of
the prophets in the beginning, did just that. However, they didn't come
empty handed. Rather, they came with proof. In fact, these proofs that
the prophets came with were so amazing that they became known as
miracles.

Each prophet sent by God had something extraordinary to show to their
people. *I will show examples of three prophets of Islam.*

Prophet Moses

During the time of the prophet Moses the Pharaohs enjoyed watching
magic. It was their entertainment and the richest amongst them

163

enjoined in marveling at the latest magic tricks. Prophet Moses who was the brother of Prophet Aaron was sent to convey one message; the Oneness of God. When Moses went to Pharoah to convey to him the message of God, pharaoh bought his best Magicians to challenge prophet Moses's statements. The magicians dropped threads that turned into miniature snakes. The staff of Moses turned into a serpent and the serpent ate the mini-snakes of the other magicians.

In the Qur'an God states, how Moses parted the sea with his staff

"So, We revealed to Musa, 'Strike the sea with your staff.' And it split in two, each part like a towering cliff. And We brought the others right up to it. We rescued Musa and all those who were with him. Then We drowned the rest. There is certainly a Sign in that yet most of them are not believers. Truly your Lord is the Almighty, the Most Merciful." (Qur'an, 26:63-68)
However, all of these miracles happened by Gods will.

Prophet Jesus

During the time of prophet Jesus many people were proficient physicians and doctors that excelled in medicine. Prophet Jesus who

164

was the son of Mary; was sent with one message, the Oneness of God.
Prophet Jesus cured the leper he cured the sick
healed the blind he raised the dead back to life Baby Jesus spoke in the
cradle when he was younger he produced a table with food, that came
from heaven.

*As God Almighty states in the Qur'an: {[And remember] when the
disciples said, "O Jesus, Son of Mary, can your Lord send down to us a
table [spread with food] from the heaven? [Jesus] said," Fear Allaah,
if you should be believers. "They said, "We wish to eat from it and let
our hearts be reassured and know that you have been truthful to us and
be among its witnesses. "Said Jesus, the son of Mary, "O Allaah, our
Lord, send down to us a table [spread with food] from the heaven to be
for us a festival for the first of us and the last of us and a sign from You.
And provide for us, and You are the best of providers. "Allaah said,
"Indeed, I will send it down to you, but whoever disbelieves afterwards
from among you – then indeed will I punish him with a punishment by
which I have not punished anyone among the Worlds."} [Quran 5:
112-115]*

And when he came as a Messenger to the children of Israel, he said, "I
have come to you with a clear Sign from your Lord: in your very
presence, I make the likeness of a bird out of clay and breathe into it
and it becomes, by God's Command, a bird. I heal those born blind and

165

the lepers and I bring to life the dead by God's Command: I inform you of what you eat and what you store up in your houses. Surely there is a great Sign for you in all this, if you have a mind to believe. [45] And I have come to confirm those teachings of the Guidance of the Torah which are intact in my time. [46] Lo! I have come with a clear Sign from your Lord; [47] so fear God and obey me. Indeed God is my Lord, and also your Lord; therefore worship Him alone: that is the straight way. "Quran 3:49-51

However, all of these miracles only happened by Gods will.

Prophet Abraham

Prophet Abraham also preached the Oneness of God. He urged his people to stop idol worshipping.
When the people of prophet Abraham got tired of his preaching they decided to throw him into a blazing fire. The fire didn't burn him or harm him, because God protected him, as God states in his most divine words;

They [his people] said, "Burn him [Ibrahim] and avenge your gods if you must punish him." We said, "Fire, be coolness and peace for Ibrahim!" They desired to trap him, but We made them the losers. We delivered both him and Lot to the land which We had blessed for all beings. And in addition to that We gave him Isaaq and then Jacob for a grandson and made both of them righteous. We made them leaders, guiding by Our command, and revealed to them how to do good and perform prayer and give alms, and they worshipped none but Us. (Surat al-Anbiya', 68-73)

(Note: The eloquent way in which God refers to himself in the Qur'an is by the phrases "We" and "Us", God doesn't us "I" in the Qur'an. The reason is because God is superior and refers to himself as a collective unit, after all he is the strong in might the powerful. These phrases do not indicate that God has an equal.

Proof that the Quran is a Miracle

A lot of the times, when speaking about the genesis of the universe and the stories of the prophet I use the Qur'an as proof of how it really happened. Therefore, I want my readers to know ahead of time the authenticity of the Qur'an and understand the reason why this book cultivated as many as 2.5 billion followers.

Every nation had a prophet and when a prophet sent by God came to that nation they came with proofs. During the time of prophet Mohamed (peace be upon him), the Arabs at the time were excellent writers, poets, and orators. Thus, God produced the best piece known to mankind; the Qur'an. It came with three challenges, and those three challenges were not met by an human being to ever walk the face of this Earth.

The Eloquence of the Qur'an

The Qur'an is originally in the Arabic language. Before the Qur'an was revealed the Arabic language was a basic means of communicating and grammatical rules weren't imposed on one who was speaking it. The Arabic language is a 6th century language and since then many of the speakers of the language never studied their language, it was just a developed way of speaking. The Arabic language was not written down by most of the population; rather the people orally memorized everything they needed to know. Stories and legends were passed down from generation to generation orally. Nothing was kept in clear record; in fact, Arabians preferred that their genealogical lineages be passed down orally.

When the Qur'an was revealed; grammar for the Arabic language was developed. That is because the way God has perfected the Arabic language in the Qur'an made way for many scholars to learn their own language in a way they have never known before. Early historians, and learned men began to study Arabic with a stride that never existed before the Qur'an was revealed. Gods speech made Arabic so rich that many books were written on the Arabic language.

The Qur'an paved way for the usage of new words. It was better than any piece of literature written by every Arabian scholar in the face of this planet. The richness of the text, the melodious structure that places ease and contentment into one's heart and the detailed enunciation of each letter was outstanding. It surpassed the writings of even the most learned man of the Arabic language, since it was revealed and after it was revealed.

The Challenges in the Qur'an

God revealed the following verse challenging the whole of mankind and jinnkind (the spiritual world); to produce one like it.

Say: "If the mankind and the jinns
were together to produce the like of this Qur'an, they could not

**produce the
like thereof, even if they helped one another." [Qur'an 17:88]**

Mankind was unable to do so and then God revealed a verse asking for
less this time; to produce ten chapters like those in the Qur'an.

**Or they say, "He (Prophet
Muḥammad) forged it (the Qur'an)." Say: "Bring you then ten
forged surah (chapters) like unto it, and call whomsoever you can,
other than
Allah (to your help), if you speak the truth!" [Qur'an 11:13]**

This challenge was unable to be met. Then God revealed another verse,
but this time He asked for mankind to produce only a chapter like it.

**And if you Arab pagans, Jews, and Christians are in doubt
concerning that which We have sent down (i.e. the Qur'an) to Our
slave (Muḥammad Peace be upon him), then produce a surah
(chapter) of the like thereof and call your witnesses, supporters and
helpers besides Allah, if you are truthful. Then if you cannot, and
of a surety you cannot; fear the fire whose fuel is men and stones,
which is prepared for those who reject faith [Qur'an 2:23]**

Or do they say: "He (Mu<u>h</u>ammad) has forged it?" Say: "Bring then a surah (chapter) like
unto it, and call upon whomsoever you can, besides Allah, if you are
truthful!" [Qur'an 10:37-38]

Yet again, this challenge was not completed. Then God revealed another verse, this time he asked for only a few short verses.

Or do they say: "He
(Mu<u>h</u>ammad) has forged it (this Qur'an)?" Nay! They believe not!
Let them then produce a recital like unto it (the Qur'an) if they are
truthful. [Qur'an 52:33-34]

When all of the above challenges were not able to be met by even the most knowledgeable in Arabic prose, poetry, literature, and writing; God revealed this final verse on this subject:

And this Qur'an is not such as could ever be produced by other than Allah; Lord of the heavens and the earth, but it is a confirmation of (the revelation) which was before it [i.e. the Taurat (Torah), and the Injeel (Gospel), etc.], and a full explanation of the Book (i.e. laws and orders, etc, decreed for mankind) – wherein there is no doubt from the Lord of mankind and all that exists.

Now, a person who doesn't speak Arabic would not understand why making something like the Qur'an would be so difficult. Therefore, I will break it down for you.

In Arabic, there is something called "The sixteen seas" or "The sixteen Bihaar". They were used for poetry in the pre-Islamic period, and is also used in poetry for the Arabic language today. They are called "seas" because it is how the rhythms of each line falls in poetry, and these were the rules used in order to make excellent poetry.

These are the names of the "seas": **at-Tawil, al-Bassit, al-Wafir, al-Kamil, ar-Rajs, al-Khafif, al-Hazaj, al-Muttakarib, al-Munsarih, al-Muktatab, al-Muktadarak, al-Madid, al-Mujtath, al-Ramel, al-Khabab and as-Saria'**.

Gods speech; the Qur'an, did not use any of these rules. Not only that, the Qur'an met all of the qualities of excellent rhyming's and it was clear and understandable speech. If a human being tried to write a poem in Arabic without using these rules, it would be normal speech or speech that is not understandable. These challenges left the Pagans of Arabia during the time of the prophet at loss. They were stuck in every way and were unable to combat these challenges. Thus, the Qur'an is the only remaining book that is inimitable and incomparable.

Alqama bin Abd al-Manaf confirmed and said the following when he addressed the pagans, Quraysh:

"Oh Quraish, a new calamity has befallen you. Mohammed was a young man the most liked among you, most truthful in speech, and most trustworthy, until, when you saw gray hairs on his temple, and he brought you his message, you said that he was a sorcerer, but he is not, for we seen such people and their spitting and their knots; you said, a diviner, but we have seen such people and their behavior, and we have heard their rhymes; you said a soothsayer, but he is not a soothsayer, for we have heard their rhymes; and you said a poet, but he is not a poet, for we have heard all kinds of poetry; you said he was possessed, but he is not for we have seen the possessed, and he shows no signs of their gasping and whispering and delirium. Oh men of Quraish, look to your affairs, for by Allah a serious thing has befallen you."

"E H Palmer, as early as 1880, recognized the unique style of the Qur'an. But he seem to have been wavering between two thoughts. He writes in the Introduction to his translation of the Qur'an: That the best of Arab writers has never succeeded in producing anything equal in merit to the Qur'an itself is not surprising. In the first place, they have agreed before-hand that it is unapproachable, and they have adopted its style as the perfect standard; any deviation from it

therefore must of necessity be a defect. Again, with them this style is not
spontaneous as with Muhammad and his contemporaries, but is as
artificial as though Englishmen should still continue to follow Chaucer
as their model, in spite of the changes which their language has
undergone. **With the Prophet, the style was natural, and the words**
were those in every-day ordinary life, while with the later Arabic
authors the style is imitative and the ancient words are introduced as
a literary embellishment. The natural consequence is that their
attempts look labored and unreal by the side of his impromptu and
forcible eloquence. "

On the influence of the Qur'an on Arabic literature Author Gibb says:

"The influence of the Koran on the development of Arabic Literature
has been incalculable, and exerted in many directions. **Its ideas, its**
language, its rhymes pervade all subsequent literary works in greater
or lesser measure. Its specific linguistic features were not emulated,
either in the chancery prose of the next century or in the later prose
writings, but it was at least partly due to the flexibility imparted by the
Koran to the High Arabic idiom that the former could be so rapidly
developed and adjusted to the new needs of the imperial government
and an expanding society. "

174

Lastly, the beautiful style of the Qur'an is admired even by the Arab Christians:

"The Quran is one of the world's classics which cannot be translated without grave loss. It has a rhythm of peculiar beauty and a cadence that charms the ear. **Many Christian Arabs speak of its style with warm admiration, and most Arabists acknowledge its excellence. When it is read aloud or recited it has an almost hypnotic effect that makes the listener indifferent to its sometimes-strange syntax and its sometimes, to us, repellent content. It is this quality it possesses of silencing criticism by the sweet music of its language that has given birth to the dogma of its inimitability; indeed, it may be affirmed that within the literature of the Arabs, wide and fecund as it is both in poetry and in elevated prose, there is nothing to compare with it.***"

Note: Mohamed (may Gods peace and mercy be upon him), was an illiterate man who couldn't read or write. This fact is known by both Muslim and non-Muslim scholars. Therefore, it would be even more impossible that he could author something as extraordinary as the Qur'an.

Time in the Qur'an

When God is reminding believers of the lives the prophets lived, and past stories; He doesn't say 'A long time ago,', 'In history', 'Countless years ago,' this is what happened'…
Rather God recounts these stories as if we were present when it was happening.
God who doesn't need space or time to exist, the ever existent; has all of these occurrences in his divine memory. What is even more interesting, is how the Qur'an doesn't put time between what happened a long time ago and what is happening now.

When God recalls past events, He speaks of it as if we were there when it was happening, as a collective human memory, and as if what happened is a part of ourselves.

**"And remember We gave Moses the Scripture and the Criterion (between right and wrong) (Qur'an 2:54)….
And remember Abraham and Isma'il raised the foundations of the House (Qur'an 2:127)….And remember We divided the sea for you (Qur'an 2:51)….And remember We took your covenant (Qur'an 2:63)….Remember Your Lord inspired the angels (Qur'an 8:12)…. This is a word of remembrance to those who remember (Qur'an 11:114) ….And remember Jesus, the Son of Mary, said…."(Qur'an 61:6).**

This method of explaining occurrences of the past; lifts them out of time and gives them a reality no other history book can do. It displays them as universal memories, and asks us to remember and recall.

God in the Qur'an ask us to be present in our own era, whilst remembering His divine teachings to us, and whatever happened a long time ago; shouldn't be regarded as tales of the ancient.

Qur'an on Embryology

In the Qur'an, God describes in detail how a baby is formed within the womb of the mother. This could not have been known approximately 1400, where there was no technology.

"We created man from an extract of clay, We later placed him as a mixed drop in a place of settlement, firmly fixed, later We made the mixed drop into a leech-like structure, and then We changed the leech-like structure into a chewed-like substance, then out of the chewed-like substance We made the skeleton/ bones, then we clothed the skeleton with muscles/ flesh, later We caused him to grow and come into as another creation, So, blessed be Allah, the best of Creators." (The Quran, 23:12-14)

A non-Muslim professor from one of the leading Universities in Canada, by the name of Keith Moore, was amazed by the simplicity in which God explains the creation of a human being within the womb. He admitted that he uses this verse in order to better explain the process of a human being creation. In a forum, in front of a large crowd he stated that the Qur'an could not have been from a human being, but is indeed a Divine Book from God.

Qur'an on babies Stage in a Mother's Womb

The Quran tells us that man is created in a three-stage process in the mother's womb.

"He creates you stage by stage in your mothers' wombs in a threefold darkness. That is God, your Lord. Sovereignty is His. There is no god but Him. So what made you deviate?" (The Quran, 39:6)

Modern science now approves that there are in fact stages a human being crosses in the womb:

"Pre-embryonic stage: In this first phase, the zygote grows by division, and when it becomes a cell cluster, it buries itself in the wall of the

uterus. While they continue growing, the cells organize themselves in three layers.

Embryonic stage: *The second phase lasts for five and a half weeks during which the baby is called an "embryo". In this stage, the basic organs and systems of the body start to appear from the cell layers.*

Fetal stage: *From this stage on, the embryo is called a "foetus". This phase begins at the 8ᵗʰ week of gestation and lasts until the moment of birth. The distinctive character of this stage is that the foetus looks just like a human being, with its face, hands and feet. Although it is only 3 cm. long initially, all of its organs have become apparent. This phase lasts for about 30 weeks and development continues until the week of delivery."*

Qur'an on all things created from Water

Scientists and researches have now come to know that everything's creation first came from the sea. In others words the sea was producing an element called 'protoplasm', this element then made a particle named 'amoeba', and through this living organism life was developed. In the following verse God explains how every living thing was made out of water.

"And We made from water every living thing; will they (the unbelievers, the atheists, and the agnostics) then not believe?" (The Qur'an, 21:30)

"And Allah created every animal from water, of them there are some that creep on their bellies, some that walk on two legs, and some that walk on four legs; Allah creates what He wills, for verily Allah has power over all things." (The Qur'an, 24:45)

It is impossible for this piece of knowledge to have been know 14 centuries ago; it is only through God mankind could have known this information at that time.

Qur'an on the Process of Rain and Clouds

In the Qur'an, God describes the process of rain. This could not have been known approximately 1400, where there was no technology.

Do not you see that God drives the clouds, then joins them together, then piles them on each other, then you see the rain comes forth from between them. And He sends down hail from the sky, where there are mountains of it. And strikes those with it whom He will

and diverts it from whomever He wills. The vivid flash of its lightning nearly blinds the sight. (24:43)

The process of rain is in every textbook and science curriculum in the United States. However, these well-known facts were recently discovered. Rain doesn't come from any cloud, it comes from the cumulonimbus cloud. Thus, the phrase; "...piles them on each other." God covered the essentials of rain and how a cloud stacks one atop another in the Qur'an 1400 years ago.

Qur'an on Black Holes in the Galaxies

God takes an oath on certain subjects in the Qur'an. In one verse God says:

And I swear by the stars' positions-and that is a mighty oath if you only knew. (Qur'an, 56:75-76)

The word "black hole" became a part a cosmological term in the 1960's. It was further studied throughout the years. A black hole is now defined as a glider, a vacuum, or a sweeping star. The phrase used in the Qur'an is 'Al-Jawaar Al-Kunas'; which can mean the following; gliding, sweeping, a vacuum, sweeper or piercing. If one researches more about black holes today on the NASA website, they will see that it matches the way the Qur'an describes it. Furthermore, God has given this entity a nickname; and a word that was not know to Arabs at the time "Tariq"

I take an oath by Heaven and the Tariq! And what will convey to you what the Tariq is? The Star Piercing the darkness! (Qur'an, 86:1-3)

Qur'an on the Expiration of a Star

The Qur'an explains the fact that the star has an ending.

"And when the heaven splits asunder and becomes a rose-like paint. So which of the favors of your Lord would you deny?
_"
(Quran 55:37-38)

A picture of a star explosion from the NASA website, the picture on the website was titled "Star Explosion Leaves Behind a Rose"

Seen as a red dusty cloud in this image from NASA's Wide-field Infrared Survey
Explorer, or WISE, Puppis A is the remnant of a supernova explosion. Image
credit: NASA/JPL-Caltech/UCLA

Qur'an on the Two Seas

God speaks of how the two seas; one salty and another fresh meet somewhere. He also mentions that the place where they meet there is a barrier. This barrier causes the two seas to stay separate and not mix.

**He has set free the two seas meeting together. There is a barrier between
them. They do not transgress. (Quran, 55:19-20)**

> **He is the one who has set free the two kinds of water, one sweet and palatable, and the other salty and bitter. And He has made between them a barrier and a forbidding partition. (Quran, 25:53)**

A person may ask why is it the Qur'an speaks of fresh and salt water having a barrier and not the two seas. The reason why is because in certain areas like the estuaries there is something called "pycnocline zone", this zone is what scientists say separates the two seas. Thus, the Qur'ans explanation; "a barrier."

Qur'an on the Expiration of the Sun and the Moon

God Almighty says in the Qur'an that the sun and moon have a specified time.

> **He created the heavens and the earth with truth. He wraps the night around the day and wraps the day around the night, and has made the Sun and Moon subservient, <u>each one running for a specified term</u>. Is He not indeed the Almighty, the Endlessly Forgiving? (Surah Az-Zumar, 5)**

In this verse, the phrase "mussaman" is used. This phrase means "appointed time", "specified time", or "specified term". This phrase also shows that the life span for the sun is not forever, and that it will expire.

A report titled "The Death of the Sun" by the *BBC News* Science Department says:

> ... *The Sun will gradually die. As a star's core crashes inwards, it eventually becomes hot enough to ignite another of its constituent atoms, helium. Helium atoms fuse together to form carbon. When the helium supply runs out, the center collapses again and the atmosphere inflates. The Sun isn't massive enough to fully re-ignite its core for a third time. So it goes on expanding, shedding its atmosphere in a series of bursts... The dying core eventually forms a white dwarf – a spherical diamond the size of the Earth, made of carbon and oxygen. From this point on the Sun will gradually fade away, becoming dimmer and dimmer until its light is finally snuffed out.*

A documentary, also called "The Death of the Sun," broadcast by *National Geographic TV*, provides the following description:

> *It (the Sun) generates heat and sustains life on our planet. But like humans, the Sun has a limited lifespan. As our star ages, it will become*

hotter and expand, evaporating all of our oceans and killing all life on planet Earth... The Sun will get hotter as it ages and burns fuel faster. Temperatures will increase, eventually wiping out animal life, evaporating our oceans and killing all plant life... the Sun will swell and become a red giant star, swallowing up the nearest planets. Its gravitational pull will lessen and perhaps allow Earth to escape. By the end, it will shrink into a white dwarf star, emitting a week glow for hundreds of billions of years. 3

These incidents were discovered recently through research, technology and astronomical instruments.

... My Lord encompasses all things in His knowledge so will you not pay heed? (Surat Al-An'am, 80)

Qur'an on Mountains

In the Qur'an, God describes in how mountains have deep roots or pegs. This could not have been known approximately 1400, where there was no technology.

"Have We not made the earth as a bed, and the mountains as pegs?"
(78:6-7)

Modern geologists recently discovered that mountains have deep roots. They also confirmed this verse, by saying that these 'deep roots' are indeed the shape of pegs.

Qur'an on the Queen Bee

In the Qur'an, God describes how the bee produces honey and how the honey can be used as a cure.

"And your Lord taught the honey bee to build its cells in hills, on trees, and in (men's) habitations; Then to eat of all the produce (of the earth), and find with skill the spacious paths of its Lord: there issues from within their bodies a drink of varying colors, wherein is healing for men: verily in this is a Sign for those who give thought.
(Surat an-Nahl (The Bee), 68-69)

Qur'an on Orbits

The Qur'an teaches us that everything in the galaxy is going in a prescribed path, or orbit.

"By the sky full of paths and orbits." (The Quran, 51:7)

"Allah is the One who created the night, and the day, and the sun and the moon, swim along, each in its (own) orbit." (21:33)

"It is not permitted for the sun to overtake the moon, nor can the night outstrip the day, each swim along in its (own) orbit." (36:40)

There are 200 million galaxies in the universe. The galaxies consist of thousands of billions of stars, and each object in the universe has an orbit.

"The sun runs on its fixed course for a term (appointed); that is the decree of the All-Mighty, the All-Knowing." (Yaseen 36:38)

Amazing; the sun is not standing in one place it also; it travels. According to science the sun travels at a speed of 150 miles per second, this means the sun travels 12,960,000 miles a day.

Qur'an on Pain Receptors in the Body

The Qur'an explains how human beings can feel degrees of burning to a certain point.
(As for) those who disbelieve in Our communications, We shall make them enter fire; so oft as their skins are thoroughly burned,

We will change them for other skins, that they may taste the chastisement; surely Allah is Mighty, Wise. [4:56]

It was thought that feeling pain was due to brain. This was later viewed as incorrect, pain receptions were recently discovered in the 20th century, when God Almighty explained it to mankind 1400 years ago.

Furthermore, burning can only be felt to a certain extent. In one of the anatomy courses that I have taken at Harvard University, for a Masters in Neuroscience program the professor described how the nerve endings on the skin can be damaged causing a person to lose their sensory receptors that feel pain.

Burning of skin depends on certain factors such as; the degree of the burn and the age of the person. There are three degrees of burns: In the first degree, the skin becomes red and experiences pain, in a second degree burn the skin has large marks, blisters, and hurts terribly; the epidermis is affected. Lastly, the third degree, burn affects the epidermis, the dermis and can reach the underlying pain receptors and destroy them. When the pain receptors are destroyed a person can no longer feel pain. Thus, God Almighty, the Wise says he will provide them with new skin so that their punishment will be everlasting.

Qur'an on the Big Bang

The Qur'an describes how the heavens and the earth were once one entity. It was indeed by the leave of God that these to mighty masses were disconnected and spread out.

> **Do not the unbelievers see that the heavens and the earth were *a* closed-up *mass* (*ratqan*), then We clove them asunder (*fataqna*)? And We made from water every living thing. Will they not then believe? Qur'an 21:31**

This could not have been known to Mohamed (may God send peace and blessings be upon him). This notion was recently stated and is now a topic that is widely studied. Thanks to God Muslims new many years before.

Qur'an on the Expansion of the Universe

In this verse God explains the expanding universe. Again, this could not have been known by any man at the time; let alone Mohamed (peace be upon him).

"And it is We who have constructed the heaven with might, and verily, it is We who are steadily expanding it." (51:47)

Just in the beginning of the 20th century two learned men; Alexander Friedmann and the Belgian cosmologist Georges Lemaitre stated that the universe is in constant motion and is expanding.

Qur'an on Sky Not Having Support

The Sky is supported by God, as stated in the Qur'an;

> **"We made the sky a preserved and protected roof yet still they turn away from Our Signs."**
> **(The Qur'an, 21:32)**

God after creating the sky (heavens) he raised it up and He explains in the following verse how the sky does not have any other factor holding it from collapsing.

"God is He who raised up the heavens without any support…." Surah Ar-Rad, 2

Qur'an on the Returning Sky

"By Heaven with its cyclical systems."
(The Qur'an, 86:11)

Here cyclical means; returning, turning, or reflecting back. It is said that the ionosphere reflects radio waves from the Earth back to Earth, which makes mass communication in the world possible today. The magnetosphere also works as a protector. It protects the earth from harmful radioactive particles that are a result of the sun. It does so by sending these harmful particles back to the solar system. Again, this shows this could not have been known during the lifetime of prophet Mohamed (peace be upon him).

Qur'an on the Ozone Layer

In the following verse God describes how he has made the sky a preserved and protected roof. This verse clearly shows that the atmosphere above is 'protecting' us from certain elements. When defining what the 'Ozone Layer' dies, one will see that it;

absorbs large amounts of solar ultraviolet radiation, preventing it from reaching the Earth's surface. The concentration of ozone in the ozone layer is usually under 10 parts per million. Also called ozonosphere. (as defined from © 1996-2012 LoveToKnow, Corp)

"And We made the sky a preserved and protected roof yet still they turn away from Our signs."

This meaning clearly shows that God is protecting us from harmful UV rays that the sun is emitting at high amounts to our surface. The subject of the ozone layer has recently been discovered in the 20th century whilst God covered it in the Qur'an 1400 years ago.

Qur'an on the Relativity of Time

As stated in my previous articles, Einstein's theory of relativity explains a lot. Thus, the reason why it is still an accepted theory even today. Part of the theory of relativity explains that as one goes further into space, the more time decreases. To us a day in our earth is short. However, once in space astronomers explain there is a major difference in the calculation of time. While they are in space time has decreased significantly, to the point that when they return to earth; they notice many 'earth days' has gone by.

"They ask you to hasten the punishment. God will not break His promise. A day with your Lord is equivalent to a thousand years in the way you count." (The Qur'an, 22:47)
"He directs the whole affair from heaven to earth. Then it will again ascend to Him on a Day whose length is a thousand years by the way you measure." (The Qur'an, 32:5)
"The angels and the Spirit ascend to Him in a day whose length is fifty thousand years." (The Qur'an, 70:4)

Qur'an on the Darkness of the Sea and Internal Waves

In this verse God describes the state of the unbelievers in their disbelief. He describes their disbelief as the darkness of the sea. When looking over the sea in the sunlight, one will see that it is sparkly and shine above. However, as one goes down the sea reaches altitudes of darkness.
Through vast research it is now stated that;

Measurements made with today's technology have revealed that between 3 and 30 percent of the sunlight is reflected at the surface of the sea. Then, almost all of the seven colors of the light spectrum are absorbed, one after another, in the first 200 meters, except for blue

194

light (picture at left). Below a depth of 1,000 meters, there is no light at all. (above picture).

This verse is from the chapter called "light", indeed God is All Powerful and the extreme in Might.

"Or (the unbelievers' state) are like the darkness of a fathomless sea which is covered by waves above which are waves above which are clouds, layers of darkness, one upon the other. If he puts out his hand, he can scarcely see it. Those God gives no light to, they have no light." (The Qur'an, 24:40)

Qur'an on the Clot that Clings to the Uterus

Another fact that adds to the topic of embryology is the clot. When the male sperm and unites together with the female ovum, a "zygote" forms. The term "zygote", is the scientific term to describe the stage of the baby when it is in its beginning stages or undeveloped yet. This form does not stay void and alone the entire time, it clings to the uterus; where it gets its source of nutrition from. One important concept to remember in order to understand the miracle of this verse is that in order for this to be seen, a microscope must be used. Now, let me ask you this; was there such thing as a microscope 1400 years ago? If you answered "No", then you do believe that this verse is a miracle.

The term Alaq used in this verse means, "to cling," or "a thing that clings to some place."

"Recite: In the name of your Lord Who created man from alaq. Recite: And your Lord is the Most Generous." The Qur'an, 96:1-3

Qur'an on the Mother's Milk

The mother's milk is a very important mixture and source of nutrition for all babies. No type of provision created by a company or major corporation can ever match the source of nutrition an infant gets from the mother's milk. God in this following verse mentions something very significant; and that is a baby suckling up to two years. It is proven today that it is the most beneficial for a baby to stop breast feeding after two years. With it, there comes many benefits and great sources of nutrition.

"And We have enjoined upon man goodness towards his parents: his mother bore him by bearing strain upon strain, and his weaning was in two years: hence, O mankind, be grateful to Me

and to your parents; to Me is the eventual return." The Qur'an, 31:14

Qur'an on the Seven Atmospheres

God describes how He has divided or arranged the heavens into seven parts. Modern science agrees that there are seven parts; naming them they are:

1. Troposphere
2. Stratosphere
3. Ozonosphere
4. Mesosphere
5. Thermosphere
6. Ionosphere
7. Exosphere

"It is He Who created everything on the earth for you and then directed His attention up to heaven and arranged it into seven regular heavens. He has knowledge of all things."
(The Qur'an, 2:29)

Indeed, this could not have been known by Mohamed (peace be upon him) then and it was not known by any man at that time; rather it was recently discovered in this century.

Qur'an on the nature of the Sun and Moon

In the Qur'an the sun and the moon are described in such beautiful terms. God calls the sun "Siraaj" or "Zia" which both mean a lamp or a burning lamp. The moon on the other hand is called "Nuur" or light, or "Munira" the only source of light or bright light.

"Allah is the One who made the sun a shining object and the moon as a light, and measured out (their) stages, that you may know the number of years and the count (of time), Allah did not create this but in truth; He (thus) explains His signs in detail, for those who understand." (The Quran, 10:5)

"We have built above you seven strong (heavens) and placed therein a blazing lamp."
(78:12-13)

"Do you not see how Allah has created the seven heavens one above another; And made the moon a light in their midst, and made the sun a lamp." (71:15-16)

"Blessed is He who made constellations in the skies and placed
therein a lamp (sun) and a moon giving light." (25:61)

Qur'an on the Proportion of Rain

In the Qur'an, God describes how rain is measured. This could not
have been known approximately 1400, where there was no technology.

"It is He who sends down water in due measure
from the sky by which He brings a dead land
back to life. That is how you too will be raised
(from the dead)." (43:11)

Modern science has agreed with this verse. It was just recently
discovered when it rains a measured amount originates from the clouds.
It is estimated that in one second sixteen million tons of water
evaporates from the earth, or 513 trillion tons. This amount of water
that evaporates is equal to the amount of rain that the earth receives. So,
this means rain circulates in a balanced or measured cycle.

Qur'an on miracle of Iron

In the Qur'an, God describes Iron was an object that was sent down to Earth. This could not have been known approximately 1400, where there was no technology.

"Indeed, We have sent Messengers with clear proofs, and sent down with them the Book and Balance, that mankind may observe justice; And We sent down iron, in which is (material for) mighty power, as well as many benefits for mankind, that Allah may test who it is that will help, unseen, Him and His Messengers, for Allah is full of strength, exalted in might." (The Quran, 57:25)

Scientists today collectively agree that Iron is not a property of the earth. That is because it would take the entire energy of the solar system to create even one atom of iron. It would take four times as much energy of the solar system for even one particle of iron to be created. Geologists today say that iron is an extraterrestrial material that was sent down to earth from another planet.

Qur'an on Subatomic Particles

In the Qur'an, God describes the smallest particle in the universe. This could not have been known approximately 1400, where there was no technology.

"The unbelievers say: Never to us will come the Hour (the day of Judgment); Say: Nay! By my Lord! It will surely come upon you by Him, who knows the unseen, not an atom's weight, or less than or greater (than atom), escapes Him in the heavens and/or in the earth, but it is in a clear record." (34:3)

The Arabic word "Zarah" used in this verse was first defines as 'the smallest particles in the universe', it later became known as an atom, since an atom is the smallest particle known to mankind. It was never known that there can be something lesser than an atom. That was until scientists recently (100 years or so) discovered that the atom can be split into two.

Qur'an on the Part of Our Brain that Controls our Movement and Motivation

In the Qur'an, God describes what part in our bodies controls movement and motivation.

"No indeed! If he does not stop, We will grab him by the forelock, a lying, sinful forelock." (96:15-16)

Why does God say a lying sinning forelock? Why didn't God just say that a person was lying and sinful. Forelock in this verse is the front part of the head; so is there a relationship between lying and the front part of our heads. Well, science recently tells us that the prefrontal areas of our brains which is responsible for certain factors lie in the front part of the skull.

A book called "Essentials of Anatomy & Physiology" demonstrate this topic very well,

"The motivation and the foresight to plan and initiate movements occur in the anterior portion of the frontal lobes, the prefrontal area. This is a region of association cortex ..."

The book further says:

"In relation to its involvement in motivation, the prefrontal area is also thought to be the functional center for aggression...."

This could not have been known approximately 1400, where there was no technology.

Qur'an on finger prints

In the Qur'an God speaks about the complexity of a human being's finger prints. There are many places where extraordinary subject are emphasized in the Qur'an. Such as God bringing the dead back to life. However, the emphasizing of the fingers and their properties remains the most significant to me.

"Does man think that We cannot assemble his bones? Nay, We are able to put together in perfect order the very tips of his fingers." (The Quran, 75:3-4)

Now, it is an established fact that each human being has a unique finger print. It is amazing that not one human being has the same pattern of finger prints. I completely understand why criminals and immigrants get finger print scans in the US to keep a proper record. That is because each human has a unique one and they can be identified by their finger prints. Before the discovery of finger prints, they were useless marks. God, has established the existence of finger prints 1400 years ago.

Qur'an on Predicting Future Event

The Victory of the Muslims in Mecca

"Allah has confirmed His Messenger's vision with truth: You will enter the Masjid al-Haram [Sacred Mosque] in safety, Allah willing..." 48:27

The prophet (Peace be upon him) saw a dream of the believers going around Masjid Al-Haram. From then, he knew that the Muslim would be able to safely return. The prophet (peace be upon him) and the Muslims returned to Mecca in 8 A.H (630 CE); years after the above verse was revealed.

The Victory of the Byzantine Empire

The defeat of the Romans was something the Arabian polytheists rejoiced in. This verse was calculated to have been revealed in 620, this was around the time when the idolatrous Persians had severely defeated Christian Byzantium. This verse was revealed exactly six years after the defeat of the Byzantium. The Persians conquered many areas surrounding Byzantium and the Arab pagans thought that the Rome's would never be able to regain their power.

The loss of Jerusalem in 614 was particularly traumatic for the Byzantines, for the Church of the Holy Sepulcher was destroyed and the Persians seized the "True Cross," the symbol of Christianity. source: Harun Yahya

Sooner or late Hercules ordered that all of the goods within all the church's to be sold to make money. That way he would use the money that was raised from the gold and the jewels for the army and infantry he was preparing. Many people and high officials were against Hercules because they knew their defeat was near and that they were on the brink of collapse. Places like; Cilicia, Syria, Mesopotamia, Palestine, Armenia and Egypt no longer belonged to Byzantium but was conquered by the Persians.

All of that changed in 622. It was in 622 when Hercules gained major victories and took over Armenia. Soon after that Hercules headed to Nineveh. There was bloody battle between the Romanian army and the Persian army. This battle is said to have occurred in 627; about 50 kilometers east of the Tigris river, near Baghdad.

A few months passed and the Persians had no choice but to sue Byzantine for peace. In a last series of battles was when that the Byzantium Empire gained its victory. The Qurayshi pagans at the time of the Prophet Mohamed denied that the Romans will ever gain victory because it seemed so impossible. The loss that the Romans experienced was a great one so they couldn't believe that they will be victorious again. Nonetheless, the prediction of the lord of the worlds was correct.

Another amazing factor to notice about this verse is the part where it says, "…in the lowest land…" When looking back at history the geographic region where the Romans and the Persians fought was a land with a low ground level. The Arabic term 'Adnal' is derived from 'the lowest part' while 'Ard' means 'base' or 'ground'. Thus, the entire phrase means 'The lowest part of the Earth.' The place where the Romans and the Persians were fighting was the Dead Sea and the was the place where the Romans gained victory.

Alif, Lam, Mim. *The Romans have been defeated in the lowest land, but after their defeat they will be victorious within three to nine years.* The affair is Allah's from beginning to end. On that day, the believers will rejoice. (Qur'an, 30:1-4)

Protection and memorization of the Quran

Lastly, God promised to protect the Qur'an from the hands of evil human beings who want to change it or corrupt it. It is a known fact that many of the books sent by God; the Gospel, the Torah, the Zabur, and the Suhuf; were lost or changed. Since the bible has undergone so much alterations throughout history by men such as Mark, Luke, Peter, Matthew, John and so on… it isn't reliable; the same goes for the rest.

However, a copy of the Qur'an from during the prophet's time can be found in a Museum, still intact and still the same as it is today. Millions of Muslims in the world memorized the Qur'an word by word and by heart. Millions of Muslims are constantly reviewing the Qur'an so that it will stay in their hearts and they won't forget it. This makes it the most memorized book on the face of the Earth. If every copy of the Qur'an was to be thrown out to the seas, it would be the only book in the world that can be brought back to its original way.

"We (Allah) without any doubt sent down the Message (the Quran), and We will assuredly guard it from any corruption." Quran, 15:9

"And We (Allah) have made the Quran easy to understand and remember, then is there any that will receive admonition." Quran, 54:17, 22, 32, 40

These miracles, is the reason why Islam the fast-growing religion in the entire world. In the 1990's Islam was mere 1 billion, in 2011 the population of Muslims has surpassed the 2 billion mark. As stated by numerous sources including the Guinness book of World Records for four consecutive years.

"Say: 'It is the truth from your Lord. Let anyone who wishes to, believe, and let anyone who wishes to, disbelieve.'" (The Qur'an, 18:29)
"No indeed! Truly it (the Qur'an) is a reminder, and whoever wills pays heed to it." (The Qur'an, 80:11-12

Quran on Lightening

It is said that when Allah orders the command to Angel Mika'eel (Michael) for the rain to descend from the heavens, he rushes to obey the command. In a blink of an eye, the army of angels working together with Angel Mika'eel gather together faster than the speed of light. Each Angel knowing his place, each Angel knowing his position, each ready to follow the orders of Allah in exact accuracy and precision. Once Allah gives the orders rain comes down, and when lightning and thunder accompany the whole seven the Angels watch in amazement and awe. They silently seek their surroundings; they could leave at once but they have so much respect for the Sovereign Power of the Almighty that they remain in position. This cycle of rain has been happening since the beginning of creation and yet the Angels are ever respectful and remaining in their reverence of Allah's infinite and absolute Dominance and Power. Allah explains this scene in the following verse of Chapter Thunder, "It is He who shows you lightening, causing both fear and aspiration, and generates the heavy clouds. And the thunder exalts Allah with praise of Him, and so do the angels in full stance watching in reverence. He sends the lightning bolts, which strike in accordance with His will, yet they argue about God though His Power is infinite. When was the last time we stopped and parked our car, just to watch the sunset or marvel at the creation of our dear Lord, in order to reflect on the signs, the universe around us displays to us.

Part 4: Life on Earth and its Stages
The First Greeting in Paradise & The Creation of Adam

The first beings to ever be created were the angels and the jinns. The angels are pure and they were created of light. They are powerful beings that follow every command Allah tells them to do. The jinns on the other hand are beings that are made of smokeless fire. They do right and wrong, reproduce, and commit sins just like human beings. At that time Allah, in is infinite knowledge; was planning to create a whole other set of beings. These beings were to be known as *Bani-Adam* or the children of Adam.

Since the Angels weren't given the choice of Will. God decided to create a set of beings that were to inevitably give the choice to choose from right and wrong. This means God prepared for us the life of this world for a purpose and as a test.

As God said in the Quran:

"I have created the jinn and humankind only for My worship"
The Holy Qur'an, Chapter 51, Verse 56

And God said to the angels:

"'Verily, I am going to place mankind generations after generations on earth.' They said: 'Will You place therein those who will make mischief therein and shed blood, while we glorify You with praises and thanks and sanctify You.' God said: 'I know that which you do not know.'" (Quran 2:30)

When Allah was creating our father Adam (peace be upon him); he breathed into him the soul. Adam quickly tried to rise from the ground and at this point Allah wasn't finished creating him; so, he wasn't able to get up yet.

Thus the verse in the Qur'an God speaks of the nature of human beings: "The human being is created hasty. Tell them, "Do not be hasty, for God will soon show you the evidence of His existence".

In the book of genesis Adam is said to be created from "the dust of Earth". In the Talmud; Adam is said to be created of kneaded mud. All similar to Islam. In Islam, it is said Adam was created of soil from the Earth (Which God refers to as clay). When it is mixed with water it becomes mud, He was molded from something akin to potters' clay.

When Adam (peace be upon him); was completely finished God commanded him to greet a group of angels that were in a congregation.

He went toward them and said the first human greeting:

'May Peace from God be Upon you' To that the Angels replied, "And may peace, mercy and the blessing of God be Upon you". From that time until now, Muslims from all over the world greet each other with these sayings of peace, taught to us through the chain of the prophets.

The Story of Prophet Adam Peace Upon him

"There is certainly a lesson in the stories of the prophets for those of understanding. Never was the Quran an invented narration, but rather a confirmation of what was before it and a detailed explanation of all things, and a guidance and mercy for people who believe." Quran 12:111

Now, the story of Prophet Adam will be the answer to why all of us are here. Prophet Adam was the first man and his story begins in the spiritual world. The beginning of Adams creation happened in a timeless, space less, and unearthly realm.

In the Qur'an God describes his decision to create new beings and appoint them as guardians and leaders of the earth. God in his infinite wisdom and might informed the angels of his plan to create a new set of beings. The conversation that went between God and the angels is explained by God in the following verses:

And (remember) when your Lord said to the angels, "I am about to place leadership in the earth"; they said, "Will You place as leaders those who will spread turmoil in it and shed blood? Whereas we glorify You with praise and proclaim Your Sanctity"; He said, "I know what you do not." Quran

"And Allah the Supreme taught Adam all the names of all things, then presented them to the angels, saying, "Tell Me the names of these, if you are truthful."

They said, "Purity is to You! We do not have any knowledge except what You have taught us! Indeed, you only are the All Knowing, the Wise." Quran 2:30-32

It was in the decree of God to create mankind and Adam was the first. However, there is one important character that everyone should know; his name is Satan. At the time Satan was among the angels of paradise, and a worshipper of God. Satan wasn't an angel, but he was a jinn (referred to in previous posts). His name is now known as Iblis, which comes from the root *ablasa; meaning 'to despair, feel remorse and grieve.'*

His original name was *Azazil.* Iblis was a very intelligent being, and after he has proven himself to God, God has given him, guardianship over the lower heavens and the Earth. All the while God knew what was to come. * As he told the angels "...I know what you do not know."

The prophet Adam was fashioned by God, when he was half completed Iblis came and looked Adam up and down. He went into his body and came back out trying to figure out what Adam was. He knew that Adam was a creation of God and he didn't like it. After that God breathed into Adam the spirit. It was then that Adam was able to get up and realize his surroundings. Adam was in heaven; he lived in heaven, ate in heaven and freely roamed his new home. Little did he know that his life was going to change soon.

Adam is said to have gotten lonely and was missing something. God in his infinite mercy created for him a companion from his ribs. Her name was Hawa or (Eve).
God says in the verses above, "…and we taught Adam the names of all things…" Adam (may Gods infinite mercy and peace be upon him) was very learned on the names of all things in the universe. The knowledge that Adam possessed was because God taught him the names of all things. When God asked the angels to name a few of what was taught to Adam they were unable to do so. It was because Adam possessed more knowledge that he gained the respect of all in heaven, except for one.

One basic moral in this story is the importance of knowledge. In Islam gaining knowledge is very important. God promised those who educate themselves and others, a high status in this life and great reward in the hereafter. There was an instant when God called upon all the angels including Iblis and he ordered every single one of them to bow down to

Adam. All of the angels obediently followed the command of their Lord, except for Iblis. Once the angels prostrated and rose, God asked Iblis, "Why isn't that you were not among those who prostrated?"

The following verses in the Qur'an explain this incident:

"And mention when We said to the angels, "Prostrate before Adam"; so they prostrated, except for Iblis. He refused and was arrogant and became of the disbelievers."
2:34-35

When Iblis refused to prostrate to Adam, it is said that he asked God for a favor. God Almighty explains the conversation that happened between him and the accursed one in numerous chapters, among them is the following:

"And mention, O Muhammad, when your Lord said to the angels, 'I will create a human being out of clay from an altered black mud.'

"And when I have proportioned him and breathed into him of My [created] soul, then fall down to him in prostration."

"So the angels prostrated – all of them entirely,"

"Except Iblees, he refused to be with those who prostrated."

"It was said to him, O Iblees, what is [the matter] with you that you are not with those who prostrate?"

"He said, 'Never would I prostrate to a human whom You created out of clay from an altered black mud.'

[Allah] said, "Then get out of it, for indeed, you are expelled.

And indeed, upon you is the curse until the Day of Recompense.

He said," My Lord, then reprieve me until the Day they are resurrected."

[Allah] said, "So indeed, you are of those reprieved until the Day of the time well-known."

Iblees] said, "My Lord, because You have put me in error, I will surely make [disobedience] attractive to them on earth, and I will mislead them all Except, among them, Your chosen servants."

Indeed, My servants – no authority will you have over them, except those who follow you of the deviators. Quran 15:28-40

Satan indeed asked God for a favor, he asked to be given a long life until the Day of Judgment. God being the knower of all that is hidden and apparent, the knower of the unseen, the wise, the perfect, the most merciful and the steadfast in punishment when needed; accepted his last favor. Nonetheless, after God accepted his prayers; God mentioned to Iblis, you and whoever follows in your path will be destined to hell. From that day forth Satan was cursed and banned from the heavens. Until then Satan will do anything to mislead any human being he can, he is out to challenge God; and it is up to us refuse all the bad he calls us to and hold steadfast to the path to God.

Iblis was indeed the enemy of our father Adam, and thus is labeled as the enemy of the Children of Adam. Once Iblis was not in his honorable position anymore he was out to ruin Adam and his new companion Eve.

God says in the following verses:

And We said, "O Adam, dwell, you and your wife, in Paradise and eat there from in [ease and] abundance from wherever you will. But do not approach this tree, lest you be among the wrongdoers."" But Satan caused them to slip out of it and removed them from that [condition] in which they had been. And We said, "Go down, [all of you], as enemies to one another, and you will have upon the earth a place of settlement and provision for a time." Quran 2:35-36

After God clearly ordered Adam and Eve not to eat from the tree they obeyed their Lord and stayed away from the tree. However, Satan found a way to deceive them into eating from the tree. He told them that they will live forever and will change into kings and queens like they should be. They were so excited by what "could happen" if they ate from the tree, and they disobeyed their Lord.

God Almighty then caused Adam and Eve to descend to the earth. There God informed them that they will stay for an appointed time. Then they will return to their Lord when they pass away. It is said Adam and Eve were looking for one another for a long period of time, when they found each other they had many offspring.

The most famous of their offspring, Habel and Qabiil or {Cain and Abel}. Adam (may God send upon him peace and blessings) was mourning the mistake he has committed in paradise for forty years. Adam didn't know how to repent, but he was feeling guilty, after which God the most merciful taught him and enlightened him. Verses were revealed to him to enlighten Adam (peace be upon him) about seeking repentance and how to apologize, and and this is what Allah says of this moment in the Quran

Then Adam received from his Lord [some] words, and He accepted his repentance. Indeed, it is He who is the Acceptor of repentance, the Merciful. 2:37

Prophet Adam (peace be upon him), was the father of mankind and a rightly guided teacher and prophet. The meaning of a prophet is; a person regarded as an inspired teacher or a proclaimer of the will of God. The reason why he is regarded as a prophet in Islam is because he was in heaven to witness that he had a Creator. Thus, he automatically new that there was a Creator and he was capable of mentioning it to his future offspring. He was also the first prophet to bring the message to mankind; so that we would know how to worship God correctly and how to ask for forgiveness when we needed it. He was directly created by God; in other words, like Jesus (peace be upon him) he didn't have a mother or a father.

When Prophet Adam and Hawa (Eve), were descended down to the Earth by God Almighty, it was because of their disobedience. Every prophet known to mankind delivered a message. Their message came with a glad tiding and a warning. When God proclaimed that Adam and Hawa (Eve) may live together in heaven, enjoy their time, eat from whatever they want; he also warned them. Their glad tiding was that they can eat from whatever they wanted, and enjoy their time in heaven. Their warning was to stay away from the tree. After having been deceived by Satan, Adam and Hawa (Eve) were descended down to the Earth.

As I stated before; in the beginning way before human beings were created, God spoke to the Angels; informing them that He will create a different set of beings; so that they may establish leadership in the lower heavens or the earth. It was decreed by God way before He even created the angels that He will create these beings to live on the earth. So Adam and Hawa were not meant to stay in heaven forever.

However, God is Just and He gave human beings the *choice of will.* This means, we have the ability to choose between right or wrong; unlike the angels who only respond to His command. Adam and Eve, had the choice to stay away from the tree or not.

Nonetheless, God is the knower of all things. It is in his divine nature to know all things, hear all things, and witness all things; since He is our ultimate Creator. One may ask, "If God was going to know everything that was to occur in this universe, then why is it that He created everything?"
We must understand that God created everything for a reason and a purpose. When God told the Angels that He was going to fashion a new creation, they asked Him; "Oh, Lord; why create something that will

make mischief on the Earth and created bloodshed therein?" and He replied to them, "I, know that which you do not know."

This shows us that our knowledge compared to Gods infinite knowledge is, nothing.

Now, after Adam and Eve disobeyed their Lord. He called to them from above the heavens and He said, "Did I not tell you to stay away from that tree, and didn't I warn you that Satan was your sworn enemy?" It was then that they were sent down to the earth and they were sent down in separate locations. Many scholars believe that Adam landed in an area near Sri Lanka and India, particularly on the mountains. It is said that from that area he traveled a very far distance, before encountering Eve, in an area near Mecca. However, only God who is the witness of all things can know the exact location of their descent.

When Adam and Eve descended to Earth, they noticed the difference between their former home and the one they were in. It was hard to make a living. If they wanted to eat, they had to look for food; and if they wanted to find a place of rest, they had to find a suitable place themselves and build it themselves. The tiring feelings of fatigue, sickness, and hardships were entirely known to them and they didn't know what to make of it.

It was told to us from our Prophet Mohamed (peace be upon); Adam, our father, was crying for forty years. The reason for this is because since he was the first human being; he didn't know what to make of his situation. That was when God the Almighty, revealed to Him; telling Adam; a few words.

"Then Adam received from his Lord [some] words, and He accepted his repentance. Indeed, it is He who is the Accepting of repentance, the Merciful." 2:37

What are these *words,* that Adam (may Gods peace be upon him) received? These words were words that taught Adam what to say to God when he was in deep regret; these words showed our father, the father of mankind; how to apologize the correct way. These words were prayers or (dua); on what to say to God when one is sorry for something that they have done. Look at the mercy of God. He created us with intelligence and great intellectual capacity and on top of that He enlightened us on the virtue of politeness, respect and high gratitude. On top of that these are all beneficial virtues that will give us the peace, serenity, and gentleness we need to live in a civilized society.

One, would say; "Why is it that God gave Adam words to use for an apology?" The virtue of politeness is an excellent gift and God taught it to mankind through Adam. Of course, since Adam was a prophet, the beautiful teachings of His Lord were given to his children who passed it on to later generations. These generations will later on, use these words among themselves; and the nature of offering an apology will be the source of creating reconciliation for many generations, and until the world ending.

We will learn later on the famous story of Adams two sons; Abil and Cain or {Habil and Qabil}; taught to us by God Almighty.

We will also learn that the message that Adam passed on to the next generations will be lost, because the new generations will start to regard the prophecies of Adam (peace be upon him) about Heaven, God, and his descent as: *tales of the ancient.*

Lessons from the Story of Adam (peace be upon him) Overcoming Hardships – List of Duaas to Make

Many of us strive to achieve contentment and success; however, given the nature of the world we live in, we will encounter hardships which will impact our ability to achieve our goals and live the life we want. We will also fail in the tests that Allah gives us sometimes, so how can we overcome our spiritual downfalls like Adam (peace be upon him) did, and learn from our mistakes and hardships in life?

First, we need to acknowledge that none of us is immune from experiencing sadness, loss, hurt, hopelessness, anxiety and/or a lack of confidence. These hardships may lead us to lose faith in ourselves and those around us if we don't learn how to manage them properly.

Allah [swt] explains to us the inherent lack of perfection in this world and the nature of trials and tribulations in the Quran in various verses when He [swt] says:

"Or do you think that you will enter Paradise while such [trial] has not yet come to you as came to those who passed on before you? They were touched by poverty and hardship and were shaken until [even their] messenger and those who believed with him said "When is the help of Allah?" Unquestionably, the help of Allah is near." [Quran: Chapter 2, Verse 214].

"And certainly, we shall test you with something of fear, hunger, loss of wealth, lives and fruits, but give glad tidings to As-Sabirin (the patient ones) …" [Quran: Chapter 2, Verse 155].

And once again, Allah [swt] in His Infinite Mercy explains to us in many places how to deal with these tribulations when He [swt] says:

"And seek help through patience and prayer, and indeed, it is difficult except for the humbly submissive [to Allah]" [Qur'an: Chapter 2, Verse 45].

Therefore, there are key elements to dealing with all kinds of trials and tribulations. They begin with our faith and trust in Allah [swt], as well as, our dua and the will to change.

Let us explore those ideas in more depth.

The importance of having strong faith in Allah

Our belief in Allah [swt] can provide us with the power to accomplish great things as it allowed the Prophet [saw], the companions and other great Muslims to accomplish what may have seemed impossible. Our understanding of the attributes of Allah [swt] – Ar-Rahman (The All-Merciful), Ar-Raheem (The All-Compassionate), Al-Malik (The King), Al-Wadood (The Loving), Al-Hakeem (The All-Wise), Al-Aleem (The All-Knowing), Al-Kareem (The All Generous) and the many other attributes of Allah [swt] provide us with a source of comfort and strength that we have The Creator of the Heavens and the Earths to take care of our every single need.

Furthermore, to strengthen our relationship with Allah (SWT), we are given the five pillars of Islam. Our declaration that there is no God except Allah and that Muhammad is His prophet is not just a statement we repeat, but the key to how we conduct ourselves in this life; our prayers are our daily source of comfort, strength, and healing; fasting Ramadan is an annual form of cleansing and spiritual rejuvenation for our bodies and souls; our Zakat (giving in charity) ensures we take care of the less fortunate in society; and our Hajj is a form of leaving all our luxuries to journey to the house of Allah [swt] to perform a once in a lifetime spiritually-reviving journey.

Next comes our belief in the six pillars of faith which are to believe in Allah, His angels, His revelations, His prophets, the Day of Judgment and fate, whether it is good or bad. Our conviction that there is a Day of Judgment where all will be held accountable for their deeds and every oppressor will be met with the consequences of their oppression and every oppressed will be met with the reward of their patience and have their rights returned, should give us comfort when we witness so much oppression in the world yet may not see relief for those who are suffering. Also, our belief in fate gives us assurance that there is nothing that can happen to us without the will of Allah [swt] as per the Prophet's [saw] hadith:

"O young man, I shall teach you some words [of advice]: Be mindful of Allah and Allah will protect you. Be mindful of Allah and you will find Him in front of you. If you ask, then ask Allah [alone]; and if you seek help, then seek help from Allah [alone]. And know that if the nation were to gather together to benefit you with anything, they would not benefit you except with what Allah had already prescribed for you. And if they were to gather together to harm you with anything, they would not harm you except with what Allah had already prescribed against you. The pens have been lifted and the pages have dried." [At-Tirmidhi]

These are all crucial elements to dealing with life's greatest trials and tribulations and returning to the path of success, and contentment in sha Allah.

The Power of Duaa

After the elements listed above, dua deserves mention on its own because the Prophet [saw] described dua as the "essence of worship" and we are told in the Quran "If my servants ask you about me, then tell them I am near, and I answer the call of the one who calls on to me" [Quran: Chapter 2, Verse 186]. We all need something in life and strive to achieve some goals – we all need faith and guidance, we all want love, we all want shelter, we all want sustenance, we all want a caring, supportive family and community, we all want to be healthy and happy, we all want to have a great vision that we strive to actualize, among many other wishes and desires. We need to search deep inside our hearts for our innermost desires and call unto Allah [swt] knowing that no dua is too great for Allah [swt], and that the power of dua is truly beyond our imagination. We may make a dua once or even for years and later forget that we made that dua when Allah [swt] answers it. If we were to closely examine all of the blessings in our life, we will realize that they were a result of our dua or the dua of loved ones for us by the grace of Allah [swt].

Having the Will to Change

One of the greatest gifts we are blessed with after guidance and faith is the will to change. Allah [swt] tells us "Allah will not change the status of a people until they change what is in themselves" [Quran: Chapter 13, Verse 11] and that

"Indeed, whosoever purifies himself shall achieve success" [Quran: Chapter 87, Verse 14].

Experts in personal development also say one of the greatest keys to success is the belief that we are not the results of our circumstances, meaning that our circumstances do not have to dictate who we are or the quality of our life. Poverty, illness, sadness, a lack of safety, a lack of opportunity, a lack of a supportive family and other unfortunate circumstances do not have to doom a person to misery. People can indeed overcome the circumstances around them, but sometimes may not be able to change due to three reasons:

1. They are either too anxious to leave their 'comfort zone': they are not willing to try something new or develop a new skill or enter a new experience because they're too comfortable and may be afraid of failure, or maybe even afraid of success!

2. They are in denial: they do not see any need for them to change and 'believe' they are fine just the way things are.

3. They tried and they didn't succeed so they lose hope.

To combat these barriers to change, once again it is important to believe that with your will which you have been blessed with by Allah [swt], you can change anything. You find people who have lost hundreds of pounds, people who have left behind an entire life that was misguided to enter into a beautiful life filled with faith and guidance and helping others realize that beauty, you find people who have left laziness and lack of productivity to build some of the greatest companies and organizations in the world which impact millions of people positively, every day.

Our achievements in life are proportionate to our level of courage, which are based on our beliefs about whether we can make our goals happen or not. So, we must believe that we have immense courage inside of us, we must believe that we can overcome adversity, and we must believe that we can achieve success and contentment In sha Allah.

And once we've ascertained that belief, it's time to take action. As we are shown in the Qur'an, belief is always coupled with action and the reward for those who consistently do good is great: "Those who believe and do good, righteous deeds, We will most certainly lodge them in high, lofty mansions in Paradise through which rivers flow, therein to abide. How excellent is the reward of those who always do good deeds!" [Quran: Chapter 29, Verse 58].

Take action, no matter how small it is to overcome the trial you are in and come back to the road of contentment and success in sha Allah, as the Prophet [saw] tells us: "The deeds most loved by Allah (are those) done regularly, even if they are small." [Muslim]".

Those actions may include:

1. Anchoring ourselves everyday with our prayers and supplications to Allah [swt]

2. Creating and maintaining a supportive network

3. Starting each day with a strong affirmative statement such as "In sha Allah I will overcome this grief/hurt/illness, etc.)

4. Remember what you are grateful for everyday – express it in your dua to Allah [swt] and/or in a journal. Research has shown that people who keep gratitude journals are generally happier and healthier

5. Take care of your body by sleeping well, eating a healthy diet filled with protein, omega-3 rich foods, anti-oxidants, plenty of water, eliminating toxins like artificial sweeteners and of course exercise, which has been shown to be just as effective as anti-depressants and

subhan Allah is a natural way to release endorphins (the "happy" hormones").

6. Show love and mercy to those around you by expressing your love to your family and friends and giving of your time, wealth and effort to the greater community – experts in happiness once again have shown that dedicating two hours a week to a worthy community effort could increase your feelings of happiness and therefore your productivity. Another beautiful expression is that if you're experiencing great hurt, become a 'wounded healer', knowing that Allah [swt] is ultimately The Healer of broken hearts and that He may have allowed you to experience that great hurt in order to empathize and be able to enable others to heal from their hurt.

7. Create purpose and passion in your life that compels you to work through and overcome your trials and tribulation

8. Finally, believe that difficult times will come to an end and that experiencing your greatest weaknesses could have enabled you to develop your greatest strengths. Believe that Allah [swt], in His Infinite Wisdom and Power, will heal your pain, mend what is broken, and grant you comfort and contentment.

Times Duaa (prayers) have the Highest Chance of Acceptance

We all have those set of prayers that we want the most for Allah (swt) to accept. Whether it's goals, wishes and aspirations for this life, or the life to come after. Or even the wishes we repeat over and over again every chance we get. The upside to this is that… there is One who is listening to all of your dreams and wishes, and knows them even before it reaches your heart. He is also so Merciful, that He has given us exact times to strive to connect with Him and ask, and in those times supplications are most likely accepted.

Below I made a list of all the times you should take the opportunity to supplicate to your Lord. Repeat the duaa's that you want most to be accepted during these times whenever you have the chance.

Before reading the list…. there is certain 'etiquette' to follow when asking Allah for anything. Allah is the Lord of the seven heavens, and all that is in between. So you are not just speaking to anyone… you are speaking to the King of all Kings. In this life it is important, to know who you are speaking to first before creating dialogue, a conversation, or even asking for anything. In this case, I would advise that you get to know who Allah is and understand the beautiful nature of the One who created you through the Quran.

When you start your duaa, first start off by calling Allah (swt) by His most beautiful names. Emphasize on His majesty, His Sublime, Sovereign and Supreme qualities. Highlight on all of the assets in your life in which you witness His Abundant Glory and Mercy.

Then begin to thank Allah for everything He has ever done for you. Thank Allah from the time before you were first Created, the time He first created your soul, the time He placed the soul into your (nafs) earthly body, the time He transitioned you from the life of the unseen, from the time you were first born until now. Thank Allah for every breath you took, every heart beat you lived through, every foot step that guided you, every neuron, tissue, cell, skeleton and organ in your body. Thank Allah for all of your senses, your thoughts, your intellectual capability, your emotions, your guidance, your family, your work, your school, and the fact that you lived another day to even say "Thank you". Thank Allah for all the things He has done for you (good or bad), those you know of and remember, and the favors you overlooked or don't remember.

Hand all of your worries over to Allah, tell Him, "Ya Allah I hand all my worries to you, set my affairs straight. Ya Rab, you know me better than I know myself help me, I need you."

Talk to Allah as if you are speaking to your own best friend. Have a conversation with Allah, express your feelings to Allah. Allah knows all of your inner thoughts, emotions, and intentions…but saying them aloud highlights your innocence, your humility and the fact that you are turning to Allah…shows Allah that you are sincere and far from arrogant. And these are characteristics that are beloved to Allah.

After that, ask for whatever you want.

Upon finishing ask Allah, "Ya Allah, if what I am asking for is good for me…make it easy for me and grant it to me swiftly. If what I am asking for is bad for me, take it far away for me and grant me what is better for me." In the end Allah knows what is best for you, so He will give you according to what He knows is befitting for you.

Then end with salutations upon Prophet Muhammad (peace be upon him), it is a respectful thing to do since the very action you are doing was the practice of Prophet Muhammad, and you wouldn't have known about (duaa, or supplication) if it wasn't for his life struggle to pass the message of God to mankind.

Once done, continue dhikr and remembering Allah. Have an open mind and heart that Allah will do what is best for you. Believe that your duaa will be answered by Allah in the best possible way. Never become impatient if you feel your prayers aren't being accepted. Becoming impatient is not the best thing to do.

Things to stay away from when making duaa:

1. Don't say "in sha Allah", Allah knows very well that everything happens by His Will and Divine Orders. Do not say, "Ya Allah, if you Will…" or "…if you wish accept my duaa." No one can force Allah to accept anything anyway, so it's kind of unneccesary to say that. Just be straight forward on what you want or need, and have trust that Allah will accept it according to what is best for you.

2. Don't ask for anything that goes against the commandments of God. Anything haram, or unacceptable, anything wrongful or anything that has to do with hurting others.

3. Don't curse others, or invoke bad wishes upon anyone.

4. Stay away from speaking ill of others, or saying irrelevant things that have nothing to with you or your relationship between you and Allah.

Things to do:

Pray for others in their absence, Allah loves that. Making duaa is a win-win situation. Whether it is answered with a (yes) or a (no), the person still reaps the benefits of their duaa.

Allah answers duaa in the following ways;

✔ Either Allah will give you what you ask for right away, swiftly, no 'ifs', 'but's or 'ands', and you will receive your request in this life.

✔ Allah will not give you what you asked for but something better than what you asked for in this life.

✔ Allah will give you something abundantly better in the life after; you will receive immense reward in the life to come, equal to the amount that you asked for or even more.

✔ Your prayer will not be accepted but Allah will transform your bad deeds into good deeds, or increase your good deeds.

✔ When it's raining, the heavens are open.

✔ When it is Ramadan, Eid, the heavens are open.

✔ When it is the last portion of the night before fajr.

✔ When in prostration, bowing down to God or in sujood, because it is the time you are closest to God.

✔ Right after you do a good deed.

✔ Right after you remember God.

✔ When it is Fridays, the time after the adhan for Jumuaa until Asr prayer.

✔ When you are crying and exceptionally sincere in your heart about what you want, throw in a prayer for all those suffering around the world

- ✔ When you finish recitation of the Quran, honorable angels surround you and they will repeat "ameen" after all you say.

- ✔ When you make a prayer for your brother or sister in their absence

- ✔ The time right after fajr, or during fajr

- ✔ When you randomly wake up in the middle of the night and you immediately remember Allah, ask for anything

- ✔ When you are traveling

- ✔ When you are breaking your fast

- ✔ While you are fasting during the day

- ✔ When you are performing the nightly prayers (qiyam); while the rest of the world is sleeping

- ✔ When you make wudu' (ablution)

- ✔ When you finish any of the daily prayers

- ✔ Right after you say, subhanaAllah wabihamdi, subhanaAllah al-adheem

- ✔ When you repeat constant salutations upon the Prophet Muhammad (peace be upon him)

- ✔ When you do something good for someone with good intentions

- ✔ When you are wronged, or oppressed by anyone

- ✔ When you are a young child (you have less sins)

- ✔ In the late nights while everyone is asleep

- ✔ During Tahajjud prayer

- ✔ When you stop something or a sin for the sake of Allah, make duaa right after

Remember, Allah is the most Merciful, the most Generous…yet He is also the most Fair the most Wise. Whatever you ask for, if it isn't answered "in time" or you feel you are getting nowhere, don't ever give up. That is something that might cause your duaa to become ineffective.

Always have patience. See the beauty in patience, and practice it wholeheartedly; by believing in your heart, mind and soul that Allah will surely give you the best. Expect the best from Allah and you will get the best in sha Allah.

Keep praying, keep doing good, grow closer with your Lord, and never give up. May Allah accept all that is good for you, and give you what is best for you. Ameen.

Best Duaa to Repeat for Good Energy

I would like to share with you one dua'a through a story which will cause a positive effect in your life starting from the night you practice it, in shaa Allah. If you find yourself not having enough energy, feeling fatigue, or getting tired easily this should help.

Fatimah and Ali, her husband, –may Allah be pleased with them- were known to be a hardworking couple. Fatimah kept her house as clean as possible, assisted her husband with his needs and used to feed the animals they owned. Whatever "automatic" machines we have today used to be done "manually" during Fatimah's time such as: washing the dishes, doing laundry…etc.

One day Fatimah, complained, Ali –may Allah be pleased with them-, about how tiring the house work has been on her. Her hands were getting very rough and she was physically getting really exhausted.

Ali, told her: "your father has received prisoners of war, so go to him and request one of them in order to provide us with support." At that time, it was a known practice that some prisoners of war could be sent to certain homes to serve them.

Upon knowing that, Fatimah went to her father's house, Muhammad -ﷺ-, to explain the situation she was in and to notify him of the dire need of having some extra help at home. When Fatimah arrived to her father -ﷺ-'s house Aisha the wife of the prophet -ﷺ- opened the door and told Fatimah that her father, Muhammad -ﷺ- was not home. Fatimah eventually told Aisha about the purpose of her visit and then she returned back home.

Not too long after that the Prophet -ﷺ- went back home and Aisha told him about Fatimah's visit. The Prophet -ﷺ- upon hearing that, being the great father he is, went right away to the house of Fatimah and Ali. Once he arrived, he sat with Fatimah and Ali and taught them a few phrases, found in Sahih Al-Bukhari, which every one of us should start practicing every single day.

-ﷺ- went back home and Aisha told him about Fatimah's visit. The Prophet -ﷺ- upon hearing that, being the great father he is, went right away to the house of Fatimah and Ali. Once he arrived, he sat with Fatimah and Ali and taught them this priceless dua'a, found in Sahih Al-Bukhari, which every one of us should start practicing every single day.

The Prophet -ﷺ- said to them: "أَلَا أَدُلُّكُمَا عَلَى خَيْرٍ مِمَّا سَأَلْتُمَا ؟" shall I not guide you and direct you to something better than what you have asked for?

"إِذَا أَوَيْتُمَا إِلَى فِرَاشِكُمَا" When you go to bed:
"فَسَبِّحَا ثَلَاثًا وَثَلَاثِينَ" do tasbeeh 33 times (i.e. say Subhana Allah)
"وَاحْمَدَا ثَلَاثًا وَثَلَاثِينَ" do hamd 33 times (i.e. say Alhamdo lillah)
"وَكَبِّرَا أَرْبَعًا وَثَلَاثِينَ" do takbeer 34 times (i.e. say Allahu akbar)
"فَهُوَ خَيْرٌ لَكُمَا مِنْ خَادِمٍ" for that is better for you than having a servant. This is a prescription prescribed to you from our Beloved Prophet -ﷺ- for an energy boost. I expect energy drink sales to drop after spreading this hadith :) Say subhana Allah 33 times, Alhamdo lillah 33 times and Allahu Akbar 34 times as you go to bed and, as some scholars further explained, you will then have more energy the following day as if you had a servant supporting you or that you wouldn't be as tired or as exhausted while doing your daily work.

243

Ali – may Allah be pleased with him – said that he never went to bed afterwards without saying this duaa even during the toughest days of his life. I ask Allah to assist you in remembering Him and bless what has remained in your life. Do your best to share this duaa with your family and friends.

The Story of Habil and Qabil

The story of Habil and Qabil are mentioned in the Quran in Surah Maedah 27-31

It is the story of the first crime that took place on Earth. When Eve (Hawwa) would give birth it was said that she would give birth to twins, a boy and a girl. Each set would be considered womb-mates, blood brothers and sisters since they shared the same womb. This meant, if you were born along with your sibling it was haram or forbidden, to marry them. The twin boy can only marry another twin girl who was born at a different time. This was to sustain life on earth.

Habil and Qabil were not womb-mates but they were the sons of Adam and they were brothers. Both of them had sisters. Adam (peace be upon him) directed that Habil marry Qabils womb-mate, and Qabil would marry Habils sister/womb-mate.

Habiils sister was very unattractive, and Qabiils sister was very attractive. Qabiil was jealous initially of his brother because he did not want Habil to marry his sister. This jealousy and resentment was brewing for a very long time. In addition, the shaytan was finding ways to increase the jealousy and enmity in Qabiils heart.

Adam (peace be upon him) loved all of his sons equally, but one day Qabiil started to notice how his father was more caring and attentive towards Habil. One day Adam peace be upon him was ordered to give a test to Habil and Qabiil. This was test was that they were to pick the best animal from their stock for sacrifice to Allah.

Now, you may think to yourself, why does Allah need sacrificial animals? The main reason was to test the love that they had for God in their hearts. Both brothers set off to find an animal to sacrifice. It was said that Habil sacrificed the best cow that he had, and made sure that it was properly ready, groomed before giving it away. On the other hand,

Qabiil coiuld not find it in himself to give away his best animal. So he gave away the skinniest, and sickest cow of the bunch.

When the time came for their sacrifice to be presented, a strike of lightening took away Habil's sacrifice indicating that Qabiil did not have the best intentions when he set out to give his sacrifice.

Adam was very proud of his son Habil, however, this made Qabiil even more jealous of Habil. He began to get even more angry towards his brother, his attitude increased, until one day he decided to confront his brother Habil for "ruining his life".

When Habiil approached, Qabiil there was a dialogue that took place between both of them which is mentioned in surah Al-Mae'dah there Allah mentions:

"And recite to them the story of Adam's two sons, in truth, when they both offered a sacrifice [to Allah], and it was accepted from one of them but was not accepted from the other. Said [the latter], "I will surely kill you." Said [the former], "Indeed, Allah only accepts from the righteous [who fear Him].

If you should raise your hand against me to kill me - I shall not raise my hand against you to kill you. Indeed, I fear Allah, Lord of the worlds.

Indeed, I want you to obtain [thereby] my sin and your sin so you will be among the companions of the Fire. And that is the recompense of wrongdoers."

And his soul permitted to him the murder of his brother, so he killed him and became among the losers." Quran 5:27-31

Qabiil confronted his brother and was so filled with envy that he threw a rock at his brother and killed him.

In that moment, Qabiil was filled with envy and anger towards his brother. When he realized that his brother was no longer on earth because of his anger and jealousy, he didn't know what to do with himself. He looked around and tried to find a way to hide the mistake that he has done. In the distant, he was show a sign from God. A bird that was burying another dead bird.

He picked up his brother, took his body as far away from home as he can and then buried him. For many days and nights, Adam was searching for Habil. As a prophet of Allah, his intuition was very strong. He felt that something terrible must have taken place, until one day he realized that his son was killed and that it was due to Qabiil.

When his wife Eve (Hawa) found out, she asked Adam (peace be upon them both), what does death mean? Adam told her, it means you cannot eat, you cannot sleep, you cannot speak, and you cannot live. She broke down into tears, realizing that she will no longer see her son Habil.

Qabiil moved very far away from home after this incident, he left the mountains and lived in the valley's where he and his descendants grew very far away from the teachings of God. Adam (peace be upon him) instructed his children who lived in the mountains not to go down to that valley, and that was the first division that humanity experienced.

Lessons from the Story of Habil and Qabiil (Cain & Abil)

1) One of the lessons we learn is the danger of anger and jealousy. It can cause division, violence, and enmity between people.

The prophet Muhammad said: "whoever believes in Allah and the Last Day should maintain good relationship with his kindred." (Reported by al-Bukhari and Muslim
Other lessons include:

- Being happy for one another, and realizing that your brother or sister winning means that you are winning too
- Developing good healthy relationships between you and others, so that you teach yourself to be happy for others, it attracts good energy towards you
- Eliminate feelings of pride and anger because they cause envy and jealousy
- Remember that anger corrupts faith in the same way that vinegar destroys honey
- Be cautious of your tongue more so than your hand because you may say something that Allah dislikes.

The Nature of Allah's Mercy

"O son of Adam, as long as you call upon Me and put your hope in Me, I have
forgiven you for what you have done and I do not mind. O son of Adam, if your
sins were to reach the clouds of the sky and then you would seek My forgiveness,
I would forgive you. O son of Adam, if you were to come to Me with sins that are
close to filling the earth and then you would meet Me without ascribing any
partners with Me, I would certainly bring to your forgiveness close to filling it."

Allah on Forgiving all Sins

Say: O My servants who have transgressed against their own souls, despair not of
the mercy of Allah. Indeed, Allah forgives all sins. Truly, He is Most
Forgiving, Most Merciful. (Surah az-Zumar 39:53)

Just as Allah is Forgiving, Merciful, and Loving; He also punishes those who do wrong, or wrong others. Know that Allah is severe in punishment and that Allah is Forgiving and Merciful. (Surat al-Maaidah 5:98)

Allah on the Pious who sacrifice their Sleep to Worship Him

They forsake their beds to call their Lord in fear and hope. (Surat as-Sajdah 32:16)

Call out to Him with fear and hope. (Surat al-Araaf 7:56)

Allah the Ever-Forgiving

And seek Allah's forgiveness. Certainly, Allah is Forgiving, Merciful. (Surat al-Muzzammil 73:20)

The Lord of Kindness

Lo! Allah is a Lord of Kindness to mankind, but most of mankind give
not thanks.
(Surat al-Baqarah 2:143)

Allah on those who Committed Sins

And those who, when they commit a lewd act or wrong themselves
with evil, remember Allah and ask forgiveness for their sins and who
forgives sins except Allah? And they do not persist in what (wrong)
they were doing while they knew it. For such, the reward is forgiveness
from their Lord and Gardens with rivers flowing through, wherein they
shall abide forever. How excellent is the reward
of the doers of good! (Surah Ali Imran 3:135-136)

Allah on waiting for those who commit Wrong Until a Specified Term

And if Allah
were to impose blame on the people for what they have earned,
He would not leave upon the earth any creature. But He waits
for them for a specified term. And when their time comes, then indeed
Allah has ever been, of His servants, Seeing.
(Qur'an 35:45)

Allah Pronouncing his Mercy and Love

"Allah's Apostle said, 'If Allah loves a person, He calls Gabriel, saying, 'Allah loves so and so, O Gabriel love him' So Gabriel would love him and then would make an announcement in the Heavens: 'Allah has loved so and-so therefore you should love him also.' So, all the dwellers of the Heavens would love him, and then he is granted the pleasure of the people on the earth.'

A God Merciful to All of Mankind

"Allah's Apostle said, 'Allah will not be merciful to those who are not merciful to mankind.'

A God who Commands Goodness Upon Parents

And We have enjoined upon man, to his parents, good treatment. His mother carried him with hardship and gave birth to him with hardship, and his gestation and weaning period is thirty months. [He grows] until, when he reaches maturity and reaches the age of forty years, he says, "My Lord, enable me to be grateful for

The favor which you
have bestowed upon me and upon my parents and to work righteousnes
s of which You will approve and make righteous for me my offspring.
Indeed, I have repented to You, and indeed, I am of the Muslims."

The Cycle of Life According to the Quran

Since Aristotle had summed up the prevailing theories in his age
relating to the creation of the embryo, controversy continued among the
supporters of the theory of the full dwarf embryo existing in man's
sperm and those of the theory of the full dwarf embryo created out of
the woman's menstrual blood coagulation (thickening).

Most of them believed that man was reduced into that sperm drop, and
they drew a figure in which they imagined the embryo as a full creature
in the sperm drop, which then grew up in the womb as a small tree.

None of both groups could realize that man's sperm and woman's ovum
participate in the creation of the embryo, as supported by the Italian
Scientist "Spallanzani" in the year of 1775. In 1783, Van Beneden was

able to confirm this statement, and thus the idea of the dwarf embryo had been discarded. During the years 1888 and 1909 Boveri proved that chromosomes when divided carry the different genetic characteristics. Morgan, in 1912, was able to determine the role of genes, existing in certain parts of chromosomes, in hereditary.

Therefore, it is clear that mankind did not realize that the embryo is created of a man's sperm mingled with a woman's ovum except in the 18th century, and only to be confirmed at the beginning of the 20th century.

On the other hand, the Holy Quran and the Prophetic speeches have confirmed in a very accurate scientific manner the creation of man from a mingled fluid-drop (*nutfa amshaj*), as coined by the Quran, which says ;

"Verily We created man from a drop of a mingled fluid-drop (nutfa amshaj), in order to try him: so, We gave him (the gifts), of hearing and sight." (76:2).

It has been agreed upon by commentators of the Holy Quran that "amshaj" means mingling, as man's water mingles with that of the woman, and this is also what the Prophet (peace be upon him) confirmed in one of his speeches.

Imam Ahmed indicated in his book "Al Musnad" that a Jew passed by
the Prophet Mohammed (PBUH) while he was addressing his
companions. Some people from Quraysh said; "O Jew! This man
proclaims that he is a prophet." The Jew said: "I will ask him of
something no one knows except a prophet." He asked the
prophet (PBUH); "O Mohammed! What is man created from? The
Prophet (PBUH) said; "O Jew! Man is created from both: man's fluid
(nutfa) and woman's fluid." The Jew said; "This is said by
those prophets before you."
In the next few pages, the embryological developments as indicated in
the Quranic verses will be discussed, while shedding light on the fixed
scientific facts in each stage of development.

The Sperm: Scientific facts, the sperms are formed in the testicles,
which in turn are created, as proved by embryology, from cells
underneath the kidneys at the back and then go down to the lower
abdomen at the last weeks of pregnancy.

Man's fluid mainly contains the following components:
the *sperms* which should be gushing, and motile to cause fertilization
and *Prostaglandin* which causes contractions to the uterus, thus helping
the transport of sperms into the place of fertilization. The man's fluid
(semen) contains also *sugar* necessary for providing energy for the

256

sperms, different fluids for *neutralizing the acids* at the entrance of the uterus and *creating a slippery environment* for the easy movement of the sperms.

While hundred million of these sperms (500 m.- 600 m.) enter through the vagina to the uterine cervix, only one sperm is able to fertilize the ovum (Fig. 2); crossing through a long distance to reach the place of fertilization in the Fallopian Uterine Tube which connects the ovary with the uterus. The distance is full of obstacles that can be compared with the distance man takes to reach the moon! After direct fertilization, a quick change occurs to the membrane of the ovum preventing the entrance of the rest of the sperms.

The sperm contains 23 chromosomes, of which one chromosome determines the sex of the embryo. The chromosome in the sperm is either (Y) or (X), while the chromosome in the ovum is always (X). When a sperm of the chromosome type (Y) mingles with an ovum of the chromosome (X), the formed zygote will be male (XY), whereas the embryo will be female (XX) if the sperm (X) mingles with an (X) ovum. So, the sex of the embryo is determined by the sperm (the male), rather than the ovum (the female).

After 5 hours of forming the zygote, which is the primary human cell containing 46 chromosomes, the dominant and recessive genetic characteristics can appear in the parent's sons or grandsons (the stage of genetic programming). The zygote is then divided quickly (Fig. 3) without a change in size and move from the Fallopian Tube (connecting the ovary and the uterus) towards the uterus, where it is implanted as seeds are implanted in the soil.

The Uterus is the place where the embryo grows and develops before emerging as a fully created and well-formed child. The uterus is distinguished as a safe place to perform this function for the following reasons:

1-   The location of the uterus in the woman's pelvis, where it is protected with ligaments and fascia that hold the uterus from the sides and allow its mobility and growth to hundred times its size at full term pregnancy.

2-   Muscles of pelvis and perineum fix the uterus in-situ.
3-   The secretion of Progesterone (pregnancy hormone) helps stabilize the uterus and slows down the uterine contractions.

4-   The embryo in uterus is surrounded with different membranes that produce amniotic fluid which the embryo swims in to protect the embryo from the effect of external traumas.

The process of fertilization and the travel of the zygote to the uterus continue for about 6 days, and the zygote keeps implanting (known as blastocyst) and growing in the uterus wall for 15 days, when the *Alaqa* (thick clotted blood) stage begins.

Reflections and comments on related Quranic verses:

"*Nutfa*" in Arabic means "very little water" or "a drop of water". This coincides with man's water which contain sperms as part of its components. The sperm or (spermatozoon) is reproduced from the despised lowly water (*nutfa*) and looks like a long-tailed fish (this is one of the meanings of *Sulalah*). Allah the Almighty says;

الَّذِي أَحْسَنَ كُلَّ شَيْءٍ خَلَقَهُ وَبَدَأَ خَلْقَ الْإِنسَانِ مِن طِينٍ. ثُمَّ جَعَلَ نَسْلَهُ مِن سُلَالَةٍ مِّن مَّاء مَّهِينٍ))
((السجدة :7-8

"*He It is Who created all things in the best way and began the creation of man from clay, and made his progeny from an extract of despised fluid (Sulalah)*" (32: 7-8)

The other meaning of Sulalah is "extract", means the essential or best part of something. By either implication, it means "part of a whole" indicating that the origin of creation is from only part of man's fluid and not all of it (which contains many components as shown above)

Clarifying the role of the *nutfa* in creation, He the Almighty says;

(فَلْيَنظُرِ الْإِنسَانُ مِمَ خُلِقَ. خُلِقَ مِن مَّاء دَافِقٍ) (الطارق 5-6)

"So, let man consider of what he was created.
He was created of gushing water" (86: 5-6)
and also says;

(خَلَقَ الْإِنسَانَ مِن نُّطْفَةٍ فَإِذَا هُوَ خَصِيمٌ مُّبِينٌ) (النحل: 4)

"He has created man from a sperm (fluid-drop) and behold this same
(man) becomes an open disputer." (16: 4).

The Quran tells us also that the essence of man is not the whole semen,
but only a small part of it. this is explained in the Quran:

(أَيَحْسَبُ الْإِنسَانُ أَن يُتْرَكَ سُدًى، أَلَمْ يَكُ نُطْفَةً مِّن مَّنِيٍّ يُمْنَى) القيامة 36-37)

Does man think that he will be left uncontrolled (without purpose)?
Was he not once a fluid-drop of ejected semen? Quran 75:36-37

As we have seen, the Quran informs us that man is made not from the
entire semen, but only a small part of it. That the particular emphasis in

this statement announces a fact only discovered by modern science is evidence that the statement is divine in origin.

The divine statement also reiterates that man's characteristics are determined and decreed in the *nutfa* stage, as He says:

(قُتِلَ الْإِنسَانُ مَا أَكْفَرَهُ. مِنْ أَيِّ شَيْءٍ خَلَقَهُ. مِن نُطْفَةٍ خَلَقَهُ فَقَدَّرَهُ) (عبس17-19)

"Woe to man! What has made him reject (Allah)? From what stuff has He created him? From a nutfa (fluid-drop) He has created him, and then molds him in due proportions." (80: 17-19).
And Allah says:

(إِنَّا خَلَقْنَا الْإِنسَانَ مِنْ نُطْفَةٍ أَمْشَاجٍ نَبْتَلِيهِ فَجَعَلْنَاهُ سَمِيعًا بَصِيرًا) (الإنسان:2)

"Verily We created man of a fluid-drop (nutfa), mingling (amshaj), in order to try him: so We gave him (the gifts of) hearing and sight." (76:2).

The mingled *nutfa* in this verse reveals the Quran miraculous nature. *Nutfa*, in Arabic, is a single small drop of water, but it was described here as (*amshaj*), which means its structure consists of combined mixtures.

This fits with the scientific finding, as the zygote is shaped as a drop, and is simultaneously a mixture of male fluid chromosomes and female ovum chromosomes.

Has anyone ever thought, before the Quran was revealed, that man's *nutfa*, when ejected, is responsible for determining if the embryo will be male or female? Has this ever occurred to one's mind? The Quran mentions;

(وَأَنَّهُ خَلَقَ الزَّوْجَيْنِ الذَّكَرَ وَالْأُنْثَى. مِن نُطْفَةٍ إِذَا تُمْنَى)) النجم 45-46)

"That He created the pairs, male and female, from a fluid-drop sperm as it is emitted."
Quran (53: 45-46),

Confirming that man's gender as male or female is determined when the sperm drop is emitted. Who told the Prophet Mohammed that the sperm*(nutfa)* with one of its types (Y) or (X) is responsible for determining the sex of the embryo? This was not discovered except after the invention of microscopes in the past century, when it was possible then to know that the embryo being a male or female is only determined by the sperm *(nutfa)*, rather than the ovum. In other words, we were in the beginning of the 20th century and the whole of mankind were not aware that the *nutfa* decrees if the embryo is male or female. While the Quran, which was revealed 14 centuries ago, has stated this fact in a very clear manner.

Here is a remarkable note! We have mentioned earlier that the sperms are formed in the testicles, which in turn are created, as proved by embryology, from cells underneath the kidneys at the back and then go down to the lower abdomen at the last weeks of pregnancy. This is in confirmation of Allah's saying:

(وَإِذْ أَخَذَ رَبُّكَ مِن بَنِي آدَمَ مِن ظُهُورِهِمْ ذُرِّيَّتَهُمْ) (الأعراف 172)

"And remember when your Lord brought forth from the children of Adam, from their loins, their seeds…" **Quran 7: 172**

This is a clear indication that the origin of progeny is at the region of the back where the embryonic testicles are formed. So, praise be to Allah the Omniscient.

The uterus, as mentioned before, is considered as a place settled (*Makeen*) and safe for the growth and protection of the embryo, according to reasons mentioned earlier. We find that Quran mentions and affirms this fact 14 centuries ago, as He Almighty says:

(فَجَعَلْنَاهُ فِي قَرَارٍ مَّكِينٍ. إِلَى قَدَرٍ مَّعْلُومٍ. فَقَدَرْنَا فَنِعْمَ الْقَادِرُونَ) (المرسلات 21-23:)

263

" The which (embryo) We placed in a place of settlement, firmly fixed for a period (of gestation), determined. For We do determine, for We are the best to determine (things). (77: 21-23).
Al Alaqa (Leech-like clot)

Scientific and Universal facts:

The stage of *Alaqa* starts on the 15th day and ends on the 23rd or 24th day, after which the embryo is gradually developed and looks like a leech, which lives in ponds (Figure 4). *Alaqa* hangs to the lining of the uterus by the umbilical cord. Blood is then formed in the vessels at the shape of closed islands, and is not circulated in blood vessels, thus having the image of clotted blood.

Although it is in the nature of human body to expel any external matter, the uterus does not reject the *alaqa* implanted in its lining despite the fact that half of the *alaqa* components and genes are from an external source (the father). This is because the region of syncytial cells in *alaqa* have no antigens.

It is noteworthy that the primitive streak is created at first on the day 14th or 15th, in which the primitive node appears (Figure 5). Out of this primitive streak, stem cells are composed, as well as the sources of the

264

main tissues of Mesoderm, Ectoderm and Endoderm, which will form the different organs and tissues of the body. At the end of the 3rd week, the primitive streak shrinks and the remnant stays in the sacrococcygeal region at the end of the spine, maintaining the remaining of stem cells in this region. This explains why some tumors in the coccygeal region which is called *Teratoma* (Figure 7) can contain different tissues (muscles, skin, cartilage, bones and teeth as well), contrary to the tumors that exist in different regions and take its toll on one definite tissue.

Reflections and comments on related Quranic verses and Sunnah:

Transformation process from *nutfa* to *alaqa* takes more than 10 days till the zygote clings to the primitive placenta by way of a connecting stalk which later becomes the umbilical cord. Therefore, the Quranic statement uses the conjunction article (*thumma*) in Arabic, indicating sequence of events with time delay and not using (*fa*) which also means "then" but indicates rapid progression without any delay.

The Quran states:

"then of that fluid-drop (nutfa) We created a leech-like clot" *(23:14)*

Alaqa, in Arabic, has several meanings:

1- A leech that lives in ponds and sucks the blood of other creatures.
2- A thing attached or clings to something else.
3- Clotted or coagulated blood.

All these meanings fit exactly with the reality of the human embryo after being implanted in the lining of uterus (endometrium), as the embryo looks like a leech, as shown in Figure 8, while clinging to the endometrium through the umbilical cord (Figure 9), blood vessels initiated in the form of closed islands giving it the image of a clotted blood (Figure 10).

A quick transformation then occurs from *alaqa* to *mudgha* within two days (day 24 to day 26). Therefore, the Quran describes this rapid change with the use of the conjunctive article (*fa*) (i.e., then) in Arabic, to indicate rapid progression of transformation:

"then We changed the Alaqa (leech-like clot) into a Mudgha (chewed-like lump"

Quran 23: 14

So even the use of different conjunctive articles has miraculous indications, reflecting the difference in embryonic stages. Thus, the stage of *alaqa* is the second stage of embryonic stages, and is mentioned in the Quran in several verses. He the Almighty says;

> *"Was he not a drop of sperm emitted (in lowly form)? Then did he become a leech-like clot; then did (Allah) make and fashion (him) in due proportion. And of him He made two sexes, male and female."*
> *Quran 5: 37-39*

And in a *surah* called *al-alaq*, i.e., a leech-like clot, Allah says;

> *"(We) Created man, out of a leech-like clot."* **Quran 96:2**

Further to the point of primitive streak, it is the first to be created in embryo, and out of which, stem cells are composed, as well as the different organs and tissues; and at the end of the 3rd week, it shrinks, and its remaining stays in the sacrococcygeal region at the end of the spine, maintaining the remaining stem cells in this region. This explains and coincides with the speech of the Prophet (PBUH) which was narrated by Abu Huraira in Ahmad's book "Al Musnad":

> *"All of the son of Adam decays, and is eaten by dust except for the coccyx, of which man is created and in which man is re-built."*

So, cells which form the tissues and the organs of man are placed in coccyx and out of which man is re-created. Verily said the Prophet of Allah.

Here a very important question arises: why did the Prophet Mohammad (PBUH) raise such a scientific issue at a time no one was aware of, and how had he acquired such knowledge if he was not bound up with inspiration and taught by the creator of heaven and earth? The answer is that Allah the Almighty knows with His encompassing knowledge that man will come to know one day the embryonic stages of development, and will know the role of the primitive streak, so He inspired prophet Mohammad (PBUH) to speak out such a fact to be a witness on the genuineness of his prophethood and message, that fits every time and age.

Al Mudgha (chewed-like lump of flesh)

The embryo is transformed from the stage of *alaqa* to the beginning of the stage of *mudgha* on the 24th day to the 26th day, which is a very brief period if compared with the period of the *nutfa* changing to *alaqa*.

This stage starts with the appearance of somites on the 24th or 25th day on top of the embryonic scapula, and then gradually appear at the embryo's buttock. On the 28th day the embryo is formed of several bulges, with grooves in between, thus giving the embryo the image of a chewed gum. The embryo turns and rolls in the cavity of the uterus during this stage which ends by the end of the 6th week. It is noteworthy that the stage of *mudgha* starts with the growth and increase of cells in a large number.

The *mudgha* looks like a piece of meat which has no distinguished structure, then after a few days, the second stage starts, called the stage of formation *(takhaloq)*, where some organs begin to appear, such as the eyes, tongue and the lips, but human distinguishing features do not appear except at the end of the 8th week. Limbs bulges (hands and legs) also appear in this stage. In the 5th week the heart starts beating and the embryo has already developed its placenta and amniotic sac.

The placenta is burrowing into the uterine wall to access oxygen and nutrients from the mother's bloodstream.

.

Reflections on Quran and Sunnah:

Mudgha in Arabic means the material chewed by teeth. This gives an accurate description of the embryonic stage as the embryo shape looks like a chewed material which constantly changes, with the appearance of somites bulges. The differences in these somites look like the "teeth imprints" over bread bite. The embryo turns and rolls in the cavity of the uterus as a piece of chewed material in the mouth.

The stage of *mudgha* comes after the stage of *alaqa*.

This coincides with the Holy verse:

(فَخَلَقْنَا الْعَلَقَةَ مُضْغَةً) (المؤمنون: 14)

"And of that clot We made a (fetus) lump." (23: 14). Of the characteristics of *mudgha* is that it elongates and changes shape when chewed. This is exactly what occurs to the embryo in this stage. As we mentioned before, the *mudgha* has an early form before the creation and formation of organs and another form following the formation of organs. The Quranic verse states:

"O mankind! If ye have a doubt about the Recreation (consider) that We created you out of dust, then out of sperm, then out of a leech-like clot, then out of a chewed-like lump of flesh, formed and unformed, in order that We may manifest (Our power) to you; and We cause whom We will to rest in the wombs for an appointed term." **Quran 22: 5**

Thus, there are two types of *mudgha*: formed and unformed. The formed one is the embryo itself which starts forming into different organs with specific functions and the unformed one is the placenta which starts developing in the 5th week (around day 35) of the *mudgha* stage. And Allah knows best.

The *mudgha* stage ends at the 6th week (i.e. 40 days). Imam Muslim narrated in his "Sahih" on the authority of Abdullah Bin Masoud that he said; "Allah's prophet – Mohammad (PBUH) – the truthful and trustworthy, told us;

"The creation of each one of you is composed in the mother 's womb in forty days, in that (creation) it turns into such a clot, then in that turns into such a mudgha and then Allah sends an angel and orders him to write four things, i.e., his provision, his age, and whether he will be of the wretched or the blessed (in the Hereafter). Then the soul is breathed into him. And by Allah, a person among you (or a man) may do deeds of the people of the Fire till there is only a cubit or an arm-breadth distance between him and the Fire, but then that writing (which Allah has ordered the angel to write) precedes, and he does the deeds of the people of Paradise and enters it; and a man may do the deeds of the people of Paradise till there is only a cubit or two between him and Paradise, and then that writing precedes and he does the deeds of the people of the Fire and enters it."

Who told the Prophet Mohammad (peace be upon him) all these facts?

Did he have anatomy and measurement tools, or microscopes to tell us the characteristics of an embryo no more than 1cm tall? It is He Allah (Who told him), the All-Knowing.

During the 6th week, the cartilaginous skeleton starts to spread in the body (Figure 12). Yet, we do not see the human image features except at the beginning of the 7th week (Figure 13), where the shape of the embryo takes the look of the skeleton.

Transformation from the *mudgha* form to the beginning of the skeleton form occurs in a very short period of time at the end of the 6th week and the beginning of the 7th week. This stage is characterized with the appearance of the skeleton which gives the embryo the human image. Reflection on Quran and Sunnah. The term of *"izam"* (bones), coined by Quran, accurately expresses this stage in the life of the embryo, which includes the external appearance and is considered the most important change in the internal structure, with its associated new relations among body organs and regularity of embryo shape.

This stage is clearly distinguished from the preceding stage of *mudgha* (chewed-like lump of flesh). Allah says;

"then We made out of that mudgha (chewed-like lump of flesh) bones and clothed the bones with flesh; then We developed out of it another creature. So, blessed be Allah, the best to create." **Quran 23: 14**

Bone formation is a notable process in this stage, as embryo is transformed from the image of mudgha which has no features of human image to the beginning of the skeleton image in a very short period of no more than few days at the end of the 6th week; therefore, the qur'anic verse uses the Arabic conjunctive article (*fa*) instead of (*thumma*) to indicate quick sequence of events.

This skeleton gives the embryo the image of a human being after being clothed with *lahm* (muscles). The two eyes and the two lips then appear, and the head is differentiated from the trunk and the limbs. This is in accordance with the Prophet's (PBUH) saying in "Sahih Muslim";" When *42 nights have passed over the conception, Allah sends an angel to it, who shapes it (into human form) and makes its ears, eyes, skin, muscles and bones. Then he says; `O Lord, is it* *male or female? `, and your Lord decides what He wishes and the angel records it. "*

After 42 nights (6 weeks), the embryo begins to take the human image with the appearance of cartilaginous skeleton, then the external genitals begin to appear later on (the 10th week). In the 7th week (Figure 13) the human image gets clearer with the start of the spread of skeleton. This week represents (between 40 and 45 days) the demarcation line between *mudgha* and human image.

So, it is well proved that the Quran's words are very well contrived and scientifically accurate, as they are composed by Allah Who has perfected everything.

The stage of muscles (clothing with flesh)

This stage is characterized with muscles encircling and tightly surrounding the bones. With the completion of clothing the bones with *lahm* (muscles and flesh), the human image starts to be more clear, as human parts are appropriately connected. After completion of myogenesis (muscle formation), the embryo can start to move.

This stage, which starts at the end of the 7th week (Figure 14) and ends at the end of the 8th week (Figure 15), is considered as the end of the stage of *takhaloq* (formation). Embryologists termed the end of the 8th week as the end of the embryology stage followed by the foetus stage which coincides with the *Nash'ah* (developing) stage as Quran stated. Allah says;

(فَكَسَوْنَا الْعِظَامَ لَحْمًا ثُمَّ أَنْشَأْنَاهُ خَلْقًا آخَرَ فَتَبَارَكَ اللَّهُ أَحْسَنُ الْخَالِقِينَ) (المؤمنون: 14)

"And clothed the bones with flesh; then We developed out of it another creature. So blessed be Allah, the best to create." (23: 14)

Until very recently, embryologists assumed that the bones and muscles in an embryo developed at the same time. For this reason, for a long time, some people claimed that these verses conflicted with science. Yet, advanced microscopic research conducted by virtue of new technological developments has revealed that the revelation of the Quran is word for word correct. These observations at the microscopic level showed that the development inside the mother's womb takes place in just the way it is described in the verses. First, the cartilage tissue of the embryo ossifies. Then muscular cells that are selected from amongst the tissue around the bones come together and wrap around the bones

The stage of Nash'ah (developing) and viability

By the end of the 8th week, a new stage starts where important processes occur. The rate of developing accelerates compared with the previous one. The embryo transforms into another creature, as the sizes of head, body and limbs start to be balanced and regular between the 9th and 12th week. At the 10th week, external genital organs appear, and the skeleton develops structure from soft cartilaginous to hard calcic bones at the 12th week (Figure 16-a). Limbs and fingers are distinguished at the same week. The gender of the embryo is manifest with the clear appearance of genitalia.

The weight of the embryo increases noticeably. Voluntary and involuntary muscles develop, and voluntary movements start in this stage. In the 16th week (112 days) the fetus can grasp with his hands, kick, or even somersault (Figure 16-b).

In this stage, the organs and the systems become well prepared to function. The fetus is ready for life outside the womb starting from the 22nd week to the 26th week (i.e., after the completion of the 6th month of gestation), when the respiratory system is ready to function and the nervous system is able to adjust the temperature of fetus body.

The first sense to develop in a developing human embryo is hearing. The fetus can hear sounds after the 24th week. Subsequently, the sense of sight is developed and by the 28th week, the retina becomes sensitive to light.

In this stage, no new system or organs are formed, and the uterus provides food and suitable environment for the fetus to thrive until the stage of labor.
Reflections on Quranic verses:
This stage starts after the stage of clothing the bones
with *lahm* (muscles and flesh), i.e., at the beginning of the 9th week, taking a period of almost 3 weeks. This is indicated with the use of conjunctive article (*thumma*) then, which denotes a time break between clothing with lahm and developing into another creature: He the Almighty says;

> *"And clothed the bones with flesh; then We developed out of it another creature. So blessed be Allah, the best to create"* **Quran 23:**
> **14**

After the development of the cartilaginous skeleton, clothing it with muscles, and the head and the limbs are distinguished, the embryo changes into a human creature well differentiated from other creatures.

During this stage, some important processes occur in the development of the embryo, which are clearly described in the Holy Quran and can be summarized as follows:

1- *Nash'ah* (developing) which is clearly noticed in the accelerated rate of growth at the 9th week compared with the previous stages.

2- *Khalqan Akhar* (another creature): this description coincides with the first one and indicates that the embryo has changed in the *nash'ah* stage into another creature, i.e., the foetus. Limbs and external organs begin to appear, and fingers and external genitalia are distinguished. Allah the Almighty says;

هُوَ الَّذِي يُصَوِّرُكُمْ فِي الْأَرْحَامِ كَيْفَ يَشَاء لاَ إِلَـهَ إِلاَّ هُوَ الْعَزِيزُ الْحَكِيمُ) آل عمران 6)

"He it is Who shapes you in the wombs as He pleases. There is no god but He, the Exalted in Might, the Wise." (3:6)

Here is an exquisite remark. Allah says in *Surat Al Zumar*;

(يَخْلُقُكُمْ فِي بُطُونِ أُمَّهَاتِكُمْ خَلْقًا مِن بَعْدِ خَلْقٍ فِي ظُلُمَاتٍ ثَلَاثٍ) (الزمر 6)

"He creates you in the wombs of your mothers in stages, one after another, in three veils of darkness." (39:6), thus indicating the

continuation of the embryonic development and the change from one stage into another, as explained earlier. Embryologists have confirmed that the foetus is surrounded, during the stages of development, with three membranes:

1- The amnion membrane which contains a fluid encompassing the foetus to make it in a state of swimming, thus protecting it from trauma that the uterus encounters, and facilitates the foetus movements for re-position smoothly during labor. (Figure 17)

2- The chorion membrane.

3- The decidua membrane.

Some scholars interpreted the three veils of darkness with the amniotic membrane surrounding the uterus, wall of uterus, and abdomen wall (Figure 18). Yet, Allah knows best.

As mentioned before, the fetus becomes ready for life outside the womb after completion of the 6th month. It is noticed that the Quranic statement indicates in *Surat Ahqaf* that the stage of conception and incubation takes 30 months;

"The bearing of him (the child) and the weaning of him is thirty months"
Quran 46: 15

Whereas in *Surat Luqman*, it is indicated that the period of incubation is 24 months;

"And in two years was his weaning." **(31: 14).**

With a simple calculation, we deduce that the qur'anic statement decides that the least period of conception is 6 months as mentioned earlier, being a scientific fact, and before the 22nd week, in which this stage starts, the fetus is not able to survive in most cases. Praise be to Allah is the Omniscient.

It is very interesting to mention that the first sense to develop in a developing human embryo is hearing. The fetus can hear sounds after the 24th week. Subsequently, the sense of sight is developed and by the 28th week, the retina becomes sensitive to light. Consider the following three Quranic verses related to the development of the senses in the embryo

(وَجَعَلَ لَكُمُ السَّمْعَ وَالْأَبْصَارَ وَالْأَفْئِدَة" (السجدة 9 "

And HE gave You (the faculties of) hearing and sight and feeling (And understanding) – 32:9

(إِنَّا خَلَقْنَا الْإِنسَانَ مِن نُّطْفَةٍ أَمْشَاجٍ نَّبْتَلِيهِ فَجَعَلْنَاهُ سَمِيعًا بَصِيرًا " (الإنسان 2 "

*Verily We created man from a drop of a mingled
fluid-drop (nutfa amshaj), in order to try him: so, We gave him (the
gifts), of hearing and sight – 76:2*

(وَهُوَ الَّذِي أَنشَأَ لَكُمُ السَّمْعَ وَالْأَبْصَارَ وَالْأَفْئِدَةَ قَلِيلًا مَا تَشْكُرُونَ " (المؤمنون 78 "

*It is HE WHO has created for you (the faculties of) Hearing, sight,
feeling And understanding: little thanks It is ye give! – 23:78*

In all these three verses the sense of hearing is mentioned before the
sense of sight. Thus the Quranic description matches with the
discoveries in modern embryology that the sense of hearing is develops
before the sense of sight

*All of the above about the cycle of life according to the Quran, is
courtesy of: Dr. Sharif Kaf Al-Ghazal (Aug. 2004) May Allah reward
him for his efforts Ameen.*

11 Qualities of the Servants of the Most Merciful

In Surah al Furqan, there is a passage (ayah 63 to 76) in which Allah the most High, describes a special group of people. This group is given a name by Allah – ibadur Rahman, the Servants of the Most Merciful, and they enjoy a special mercy from the Most Merciful. Allah describes in this passage what it takes to be an Abd Ar-Rahman, the qualities which distinguish this special group of people.

Easy-going

And the servants of the Most Merciful are those who walk upon the earth easily

Forbearance

"and when the ignorant address them [harshly], they say [words of] peace…"

When someone makes fun of them, insults them or hurts them, they don't strike back or seek revenge. They forgive and overlook. They have this attitude towards disbelievers who insult them. Then imagine how much more leniently we should behave to our believing brothers and sisters.

Many of the People of the Scripture wish they could turn you back to disbelief after you have believed, out of envy from themselves [even] after the truth has become clear to them. So pardon and overlook until Allah delivers His command. Indeed, Allah is over all things competent. [2:109]

Devotion in Tahajjud
And those who spend [part of] the night to their Lord prostrating and standing [in prayer]

The Prophet said:

The best month for observing Saum (fasting) next after Ramadan is the month of Allah, the Muharram; and the best Salat (prayer) next after the prescribed Salat is Salat at night (Tahajjud prayers). [Muslim]

Fear of Allah's Punishment

And those who say, "Our Lord, avert from us the punishment of Hell. Indeed, its punishment is ever adhering; Indeed, it is evil as a settlement and residence."

For these people, Hellfire is not a theoretical concept, but a reality.

Moderation

And [they are] those who, when they spend, do so not excessively or sparingly but are ever, between that, [justly] moderate

Allah says in another verse (translation):

O children of Adam, take your adornment at every masjid, and eat and drink, but be not excessive. Indeed, He likes not those who commit excess. [7:31]

On the other hand, we shouldn't be miserly to the point of harming ourselves and our families.

Leaving sins

And those who do not invoke with Allah another deity or kill the soul which Allah has forbidden [to be killed], except by right, and do not commit unlawful sexual intercourse. And whoever should do that will meet a penalty. Multiplied for him is the punishment on the Day of Resurrection, and he will abide therein humiliated

Tawbah

Except for those who repent, believe and do righteous work. For them Allah will replace their evil deeds with good. And ever is Allah Forgiving and Merciful. And he who repents and does righteousness does indeed turn to Allah with [accepted] repentance.

Leaving lying

And [they are] those who do not testify to falsehood

The Prophet said:

I guarantee a house in the surroundings of Paradise for a man who avoids quarrelling even if he were in the right, a house in the middle of Paradise for a man who avoids lying even if he were joking, and a house in the upper part of Paradise for a man who made his character good. [abu Dawud]

Remain away from evil conversation

and when they pass near ill speech, they pass by with dignity.

Accept admonition

And those who, when reminded of the verses of their Lord, do not fall upon them deaf and blind.

Turning to Allah

And those who say, "Our Lord, grant us from among our wives and offspring comfort to our eyes and make us an example for the righteous."

Conclusion

At the end of this passage, Allah mentions the reward of the Ibadur Rahman:

Those will be awarded the Chamber for what they patiently endured, and they will be received therein with greetings and [words of] peace. Abiding eternally therein. Good is the settlement and residence.

The Journey of the Soul through the 4 Worlds

From the beginning of time many tried understanding the nature of the soul. Many attempted to explore and gain knowledge of the power and mysteries of the soul. It's safe to say all who have even claimed to have complete spiritual knowledge and guidance have failed to do so. Allah Almighty says in the Qur'an;

"They ask you [O Muhammad (saws] concerning the Ruh (Soul). Say: 'It is one of the things, the knowledge of which is only with my

Lord. And of knowledge, you (mankind) have been given very little." [Qur'an Al-Isra 17: 85]

This verse from the most Knowing and Wise clearly states that the complete knowledge of the soul is only with Him. It is due to the fact that there is so little knowledge of the soul that it has become unusual to even speak too much about within scholastic and scholarly circles. However, there is a work done by Ibn Al-qayyim who has wrote about the soul in his book called 'Kitab-Al-Ruh'. Many scholars suspect that he has wrote this piece before his meeting with Sheikh Ibn-Taymiyah (may Gods peace and blessings be upon him). Nonetheless, it is a book written by a well-known scholar who has made his mark in the Islamic world of knowledge. Although, I would imagine the best we can do as Muslims is respect the scholarly work of Ibn Al-qayyim while also knowing that all perfection is to Allah Almighty, and to accept the fact that only Allah has the most precise ilm' or knowledge of the soul.

In my short and humble contribution, I would like to admit that all mistakes I may have made in this piece are from my own. And that Allah (swt) is the most perfect and exalted in every way.

So, what do we know about the soul, from what the Almighty has explained to us through His final message to mankind?

289

A soul is the creature of Allah. Into every human being it is blown, when it is just a fetus at 120 days old. During this time, it remains inside the given body of the human being throughout its entire life on earth. At the time of the death it departs from the body to its final destination; wherever Allah chooses for it to be. Some reside in the heavens, others at the gates of heaven, others their graves are made for them a resting place and an eternal abode. It is due to their deeds that they will be in specific situations, our actions and daily scenes of this life will determine where the end of our journey will take us.

Like everything else in this universe, the soul is the creation of Allah but as the above verse states mankind has been given very limited knowledge concerning it.

When a body is given a soul life begins, and when the soul leaves the body, life ends and death begins. Many people assume since they see the body and it is no longer interacting with its environment, it is the end for it. Death is not the end. Death is just a gate to the next realm of the human's counterpart; the soul.

In other words, the human body is a physical design fashioned by Allah (swt) to envelope our souls. This means we are our 'soul'. We are placed into our bodies to flourish and pursue the life of this world, once it is time for us to go our bodies are left on this earth to vanish and decay. We take with us one reality. A reality that has always been a part of us. That is a part of us is our souls. Once we take our actual form that will be the moment of final certainty where one is greeted with an eternity of true happiness and bliss, or a period of condemnation and correction for the wrongs committed in this world.

The four worlds

There are four worlds that Allah (swt) explains to us in the Qur'an.

1) The womb – where the soul joins its body. This world is called 'Silatul-Rahim' or the place of Mercy. It is where the body and soul are both pure and innocent. In the beginning the body and soul do not meet, they are apart for a certain period. Before the soul is placed into the body, the body itself has a name. It is called 'jismul-insaan '. The soul is called, 'al-ruh '. Once the body and soul join together as one it is called, 'nafs' or the 'self'. It isn't until the body reaches the stage of becoming a fetus that the soul is blown into it.

This is stated in the following Sahih Hadith of the Prophet Muhammad (May God's everlasting Mercy be bestowed upon him); After the soul is blown into the body, from this point on until it enters the life of this world, the body and soul will be inseparable. It isn't until death is decreed upon the body that the soul is released from the flesh surrounding it.

2) This world – where we all live for a limited period only. This world can be discussed in intimate detail, from the rising and setting of the sun; the illuminated sky situated above, the mountains standing tall and regal like and the distant stars shining from

3) The grave – a 'Barzakh' period. Barzakh means 'Barrier'. It is known as the point of no return, where the soul will stay until the hereafter. This realm is called 'Barzakh' or 'Barrier' because once the soul enters, it can no longer return to the worldly realm of this life. It is blocked from entrance of both this life and the entrance of its final destination. It is also called the point in-between. This is because it is the portal from this life and its door is the destination to the next…

4) The Hereafter – The final destination of all human beings. Where the judgment will take place, and the final decision on where the 'nafs' will go will be announced.

Each world is greater than the last. It must be emphasized that the final world of the hereafter is the greatest and the most important. For us human beings, it is difficult to comprehend or understand the sheer temporary nature of this life and the permanence of the hereafter.

Among us, thousands are buried every single day and we sometimes find it impossible to envision the new journey that the 'ruh' or soul is destined to go through. To all of us who are alive the grave is just an empty hole underground, with no signs of another world being surrounded by the body. However, to the dead, that dark hole is their window to paradise or hell. It is because human beings cannot comprehend the next life that they refuse to believe in Allah. Nonetheless, as humans we must understand the the body is not the 'ruh' or soul. The body is considered one of the things that a person has left behind on this earth; along with their families, wealth, and home.

In this exact situation, we as intellectual human beings can be compared to the fetus in a mother's womb. Consider the unborn child. The only home he is familiar with for nine months is a dark and cramped place where it receives warmth, nourishment, and space to grow. Imagine if the 'nafs' of this world can speak to the fetus. Imagine if it can decipher our message clearly and concisely. What would we say? We would speak about the vast and endlessly blue sky as our rooftop, the cascading and flowing rivers as our source of nourishment, the high and royal mountains as our strength and iron in this enormous universe, the deep blue open seas, the speed of light and cars, the sound of thunder and the spark of lightening, lush gardens filled with welcoming scents, wide deserts with unbearable heat, and green rain forests with a calming breeze, the colors, textures, and even the taste of chicken. Describing all of the beautiful, good, and bad things about the world to the fetus will cause it to listen and try to understand. However, because it has never been to the world yet it can never fully come to terms with exact knowledge of this world. The soul can only try take what we say and believe in it until it can see for itself, the many promises we made to it.

Would the infant crawled up in the mother's womb understand the message? Of course not. The only place he knows is his mother's womb. To imagine the outside world would be beyond his comprehension. What about us? Allah has given us the intellect to understand and use logic, and then he has given us the signs of this world, and then he has gifted us with His message. It is up to us whether we decide to take that message, believe in it and follow it or simply let it go because we cannot understand the complexities of its nature and foolishly decide not to follow its guidance and excellence. In simple words, just because we cannot envision the life of 'Barzakh' does not mean it does not exist.

So, what is the soul? From the Sunnah and Qur'an very little is discussed about this topic. Imam Ibn Al-Qayim wrote in his scholarly work the following;

" Ruh is an entity which differs totally from the physical body. It is a subtle, ecclesiastical, enlightened living and moving body which penetrates into the depths of the organs and flows into them like the water in the rose or the oil in the olive or the fire in the coal. As long as these organs remain able to accept the impressions of this subtle body, the 'Ruh' remains attached to these organs and provides them with feeling and movement. But when these organs are spoiled because of the dominance of diseased elements upon it, and they are no longer able to accept the impressions of the soul, it leaves the body and heads towards the world of the souls. "

The way 'al-ruh' and 'al-nafs' are used are different. The ruh is a subtle and simple spirit that resides in the heavens. It needs a physical body to carry with it on the earth. When the spirit or ruh is given a body, life begins and it is called nafs. In the Qur'an nafs is used in a number of ways, all of these times it is used in the Qur'an it is used to describe the meaning of a soul with a body.

Nafs' meaning 'self'. As seen in the following verse;

"You know what is in my self but I do not know what is in Your self" (Qur'an Al-Ma'ida 5:116)

Nafs meaning 'blood'. As seen in this following verse;

"The (insect) which has flowing Nafs (blood)."

Nafs as a strong-willed force in man, which has the ability to push him to good or evil. As seen in the following verses in the Qur'an

1) Nafsul-Ammaratun-bisuu'- the soul that dictates evil.

"And I do not free myself from blame. Indeed, the human self is inclined to evil, except when my Lord bestows His Mercy (upon whom He wills). Indeed, my Lord is Forgiving, Merciful." (Qur'an Yusuf : 53)

2) Nafsul-Lawwama- the self-reproaching soul.

"I do call to witness the Resurrection Day. And I do call to witness the self-reproaching Soul." (Qur'an Al Qiyamah: 1-2) 3) Nafsul-Mutma'ina- The satisfied soul. "To the righteous it will be said, 'Oh reassured soul, return to your lord well pleased, and pleasing to Him. And enter among my righteous servants, and enter my paradise." (Qur'an Al-Fajr 27-30)

Two deaths and two lives

The Qur'an mentions two deaths and two lives given to us by Allah in the following verses;

"How can you reject faith in Allah, seeing that you were dead and He gave you life. Then He will cause you to die, then He will bring you to life, then to Him will be your return." (Qur'an Al-Baqarah 2: 28)

"They will say: Our Lord, twice have You given us death and twice have You given us life…" (Qur'an Al Mumin: 11)

When the soul is first created it has no physical body and is considered to be a dead creature. In this state, it is referred to as 'Ruh', and this is the first death as even death is created by Allah. Stated by Allah in the following verse;

"He is the one who created Death and life in order that He may try which of you is best in deeds , and He is the Exalted, the Forgiving." (Qur'an Al Mulk 67: 2)

The Qur'an also tells us that all the souls of mankind were created before the creation of Adam and were asked to testify to the Lordship of Allah.

"When your Lord drew forth from the loins of the children of Adam their descendants, and made them testify concerning themselves: 'Am I not your Lord?'. They said, 'Yes, we do testify.' This lest you should say on the Day of Judgement: 'We were not aware of this.'" (Qur'an Al A'raaf :272)

The first life begins when the soul is breathed into an embryo in the womb of its mother, and now the soul is referred to as 'Nafs'. The word Nafs is also used for 'blood', as long as blood surges healthily through the body, there will be life in that body.

The second death occurs when the soul leaves the body at the end of its appointed time on earth.

"Every Nafs (soul) shall taste death..." (Qur'an Aal Imran 3: 185)

The Nafs dies and is buried, while its soul soars up to the heavens. That is why the Prophet (saws) taught us: "At death, the eyes follow the departing soul, so close the eyes." The second life will be the eternal life beginning on the Day of Judgement when the bodies will be resurrected and their souls will be blown into them once again. (From my dear brothers at www.missionislam.com)

So, this is a simple and summarized version of the journey of the soul. Insha'Allah to all of the viewers of this page, there will be another detailed version sometime soon. Our souls are a part of us, and it is up to us whether we want to abandon it by indulging it in harmful actions, or protect it like we would grow roses in a garden by feeding it all of the elements that will make it become sweet, beautiful, brilliant, radiant, and shining before we finally meet our Lord and Maker.

Part Five: Personal Lessons and Insight from Me

Advise to my Sisters

I want you to know that you are different. You are different, because you have been chosen, to tread on a long journey that only the general of a great army can handle. What I mean is, you will be at war with your spirit and within your physical reality. In the arena of your heart, there will battle the factions of pride and humility, ego and virtue, contentment and displeasure – and some days one will win over the other. There are parts of you that you cannot escape, flaws, and qualities that make up who you are; the sooner you accept your nature the better quality of life you will have. The Quran describes life as an illusion because you are constantly perceiving what the world expects of you, whilst forgetting about your true nature. In order to balance this, you have to accept yourself as you are, love yourself, and enjoy your own company.

You are beginning to understand, aren't you? That the whole world is inside you, in your perspectives and in your heart. That to be able to find peace, you must be at peace with yourself first. And to truly enjoy life, you must enjoy who you are. And once you learn how to master this, you will be protected from everything that makes you think you can't go on, with this gift of recognizing yourself, even when you're alone, you will never be lonely.

Second, I hope you learned: if your path is more difficult it's because your calling is more higher. Do not give up on yourself, because you have come too far for you to stop everything you are working towards. I hope you take the time to understand yourself, and become self-aware before you chase relationships with others. You are your first best friend, after Allah of course. There will be days where you will feel empty, broken, or even lost. In those moments, please remember that you are not alone. If you have to cry about it, do it, but for one day and then promise yourself that is the last time you feel bad for yourself, and that you will keep moving on,

Every day is like an empty canvas, where you have the chance to paint whatever it is you like to manifest for your day. You are the one who can make or break your day, no one else.

Set daily goals, wake up earlier, and enjoy the rays of sunlight dancing across your room. There is this place everyone created in their mind called the future, and some people are stuck living there, and it is not a fun place to be. In that place, all they think about is things that didn't happen yet, and it makes them forget about the things they can do now.

Maybe you really want a vacation, but who said you can't experience your own vacation by exploring what your city has to offer, by going to that coffee shop you've always wanted to go to and by enjoying the scenery you've been ignoring for so long – that is right in front of you. Take yourself out to dinner, go watch that movie you've always wanted to see, get a massage, or on a self-care retreat (and you can even do these things at home).

You have so much to live for, so much purpose within you that you haven't tapped into yet, why not explore that and for the first time in your life reject every negative thought in your head that has been bringing you down.

Keep a journal, write down your thoughts, organize your thought patterns so that you grow to think more positive. Did you know that positive thinking even affects our DNA? The more stressed you are, the more you will carry this energy to your offspring, who will also experience it in their lives.

When you strengthen your body, you are strengthening a whole generation of people who will come after you too. My sisters, remember that this life is short.

Life is literally 4 Quarters

1. 20
2. 20
3. 20
4. 20

The average human life is 65-70, now many of you who are reading this book are in between stage 1-2. You have 2 more stages left, and so why not take advantage of this fleeting time on earth, to really get connected to what's more important: your soul, and learn more about your origin (contained in this book) and who you are, so you can go back to God in the most elevated position.

Every good that you do, and even how good you treat yourself, elevates you. The good you do is light for your soul, the more you do it, the more your soul radiates before you go back to Allah.

Take it easy, be easy on yourself. Why are you so kind to others, but so hard on yourself? Take it day by day, go and buy a planner and write down all the things you want to accomplish this year. Take it step by step, progress is still progress even if it is slow.

This world is meant for you, you belong here. You need to start walking on earth with purpose, and full confidence – because I know there are many of you who probably feel like you don't belong because of the rhetoric people put out there about Islam and women who wear hijab.

You need to let go of all the negative beliefs that they want you to belief, and start being confident. If you are going to wear the hijab, wear it unapologetically, and with full pride and high esteem.

You are a queen, Allah's princess on earth, and let me tell you something: not everyone will enter Jannah, and it is the Greatest form of creation ever made. The same way not everyone will have access to you, so if there's moments in your life where you lose people or don't gain some of the things you want – Allah is limiting the worlds access to you - He is your protector and best friend, keep that in mind.

Remember that you will fail many times before you succeed, and so never give up, keep going. We have this thing, in our separate cultures (Africans, Asians/Arabs and maybe even other cultures), where us women put time limits on ourselves.

We feel like we have to finish school at a certain time, get married at a certain time, have kids at a certain time, and that is such a stressful way to live, don't you think? Stop putting the limitations of time over yourself, and just enjoy the process of where you are now. When was the last time you did that?

I think you owe it to yourself to just let go of all the negative things you think about yourself and embrace yourself. It is okay to not like certain things about yourself, that doesn't mean you don't love yourself. For example, I might not like the way I smile, but that doesn't mean I don't love myself.

There will be things you will not like, but you are still you, and now is the time to embrace them, and just bun what anyone else or society thinks.

If I can talk the old Amal, this is exactly what I would tell her. To live in the moment, and feel every blessing that comes her way, because time is fleeting, and this is it; this is life, there is nothing else to it. There was no trailer or pre-show features, you are just thrown into this thing called life, and all you have to do is make the most of it.

Today's Hijabi Beauty Standards

There are so many fashionistas today who are representing hijab in the beauty industry. Now, I am not here to talk about whether this is haram or that is halal. I am here to state straight facts.

The younger girls from the younger generation, obviously need high caliber influencers who are guided, to look up to. I think it is better for younger girls to stumble upon an influencer who promotes the correct hijab, then to lack that representation and to take low vibrational content – as an example.

It is essential, that influencers also take into account that they have younger people who look up to them, and will be inspired by the content that they put out. It is good to keep these things in mind as you start to become more famous.

Second, I think it is an oxymoron to widely promote your body and face everywhere while believing in and wearing the hijab. The hijab represents one thing, and many of these modeling industries do not represent what the hijab represents. So, it becomes a challenge because things that go against a sister's beliefs may be required of her in her modeling career. So, it's best to really keep these things in mind, and remember that you are not defined by the societal standards of beauty, that people expect you to meet.

You are above and beyond that, a queen who does not need other people's approval. The more you believe this, the better quality your life will be. The more you live to please creation, the lower your vibration, and the lower the quality of your life.

Love Yourself

Loving yourself, is loving Allah – loving yourself is just as vital when it comes to faith. When you love your being, you are in return being grateful to Allah for all the favors you've been given.

The body is as ephemeral as this world, as viable as a candle – it is brief and temporary. There might be a voice in your head, a moment of self-doubt where you feel you are not deserving of life and the eternity promised. But you are wrong. Allah assures us in the Quran that humans are the best of creation. That our body has been created in the most excellent form. That our conscious is from an eternal spirit that Allah has blown into us, that will live on for eternity.

It only makes sense to take care of this gift, mentally, emotionally and spiritually. To regard our time as sacred, and our space as sacred by choosing carefully who we allow into it.

This won't prove to be an easy journey, because within the arena of your heart there battles the factions of love and hate; intolerance and benevolence; self-assurance and self-doubt, but I think this is why the reward is so great in the end. The ones who overcome will be rewarded with virtues that are the keys to entering paradise.

Lastly, keep in mind that your soul is greater than this world and everything in it. The number one goal of Azazeel, Iblees, the devil is to increase in your eyes, the value of temporal things, and take away the insight you have about yourself and your self-power – all that is within you.

Every messenger of God from Jesus to Moses, and David to Muhammad, taught one thing – to keep the world in one hand, but also hold onto your connection with Allah in the other, balance is key.

Your power isn't through your money, looks, body, degrees, titles or what you gain in this temporary world. It lies in your spirit; the key is to make sure we aren't distracted and forget this. In return, this self-knowledge will raise you in status (in the heavens and maybe on earth) and gift you with serenity.

Positive Thinking

Many of you may be familiar with Dr. Masaru Emoto's water experiments, where he exposed water to different words, music, names, prayers, blessings, etc., and then photographed the way the water crystallized when frozen. Here's an example:

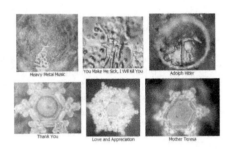

Heavy Metal Music   You Make Me Sick, I Will Kill You   Adolph Hitler

Thank You   Love and Appreciation   Mother Teresa

These experiments continue to fascinate me, so I decided to replicate them in my own way – with plants.

Dr. Masaru Emoto, a researcher and alternative healer from Japan has given the world a good deal of evidence of the magic of positive thinking. He became famous when his water molecule experiments featured in the 2004 film, What The Bleep Do We Know? His experiments demonstrate that human thoughts and intentions can alter physical reality, such as the molecular structure of water. Given that humans are comprised of at least 60% water, his discovery has far reaching implications, can anyone really afford to have negative thoughts or intentions?

The rice experiment is another famous Emoto demonstration of the power of negative thinking (and conversely, the power of positive thinking). Dr. Emoto placed portions of cooked rice into two containers. On one container, he wrote "thank you" and on the other "you fool". He then instructed school children to say the labels on the jars out loud every day when they passed them by. After 30 days, the rice in the container with positive thoughts had barely changed, while the other was moldy and rot.

Examples of this experiment can also be found conducted by people on YouTube.

This is not far off from the facts we know about plants from the Quran and Sunnah.

We are taught by Allāh that plants and several from His creation communicate with one another, and have intricate systems in which they express themselves. The Quran also has an entire surah named after ants, Surah "An-Naml" and mentions the ant that warned other ants of King Suleiman's approaching army.

Their reaction to the adverse effects of negative thoughts, show that negative thoughts don't just disappear. They are an energy that encompasses a person and consumes them.

This is why our nafs (our own self/mind) can be the greatest enemy.

Knowing this, and realizing the importance of positive thinking take a hold of your thoughts and consciousness before it takes a hold of you. Positive thinking is powerful, more powerful than you realize.

Losing Loved Ones

I remember losing my aunt, grandmother, and sister all in the same two years. It wasn't easy. It will not be easy losing someone you love and had great times with. However, what helped me is realizing that I am alive to make more duaa for them and to do good things for them that will help elevate their status in the next world. They are not alive to do good deeds but I am alive to carry on their legacy.

So always remember, you have a huge purpose now! Your purpose is to make sure the legacy of the people you love continues to live on and there is so many ways to do that. To give someone a copy of the Quran in their name, to give in charity in their name, and to make sincere duaa that Allah opens all gates of paradise for them and forgives their sins. One day when you are reunited they will remember the great things you did when they went on to the next world. Keep this in mind, and keep your head up.

What to do if you Lose a Close Friend due to "Petty" Circumstances

There are so many people I still love and have great memories with, but due to life circumstances we've outgrown one another. It may be that a close friend you always used to see moves to another country and gets married, it may be that you and another friend move for school. Everyone has a specific time frame, a journey that they partake in within your life, and once that journey is over, so is their time with you on earth – or who knows, maybe you can reunite again, if not in this world, insha'Allah in the next.

The first fact is that: people react to you based on their own capacity of understanding. If they are loud, angry, arrogant, prideful, have an inflated ego, and are unable to communicate their problems to you efficiently, those are all low vibrational characteristics.

A true friend is someone who knows how to put their pride and ego aside, in order to save the relationship you guys have been building for a really long time. If a friend cannot do that, then was the friendship real to begin with?

Communication is real in every relationship, and unfortunately many people come from backgrounds where they suffered traumas that have impaired their ability to communicate efficiently. All you have to do is always be graceful in every situation, so that once they grow and become more wise, in later years of life, they will remember you. They will remember you for the right reasons if you are always kind. Second, this does not mean you should let people walk all over you. This means, you listen to their concerns, and be concise in how you explain yourself, while keeping into understanding their emotions or any hurt they may be feeling.

Always keep in mind that people take time to heal from whatever happened between you, as long as you do your part and apologize you are good. If they accept it or not it is up to them, but at least you have a clean slate and Allah will be your witness that you offered an apology.

Now, if someone has wronged you in any situation, remember that you have the ball in your court but that doesn't mean you should go on a power trip and treat an old friend badly. Communicate, communicate, communicate – exactly how you feel and then let them know that you are free of any resentment towards them. Purifying your heart in this world away from low vibrational feelings is essential to a better lifestyle.

Remember if you lose someone in this life, that just means their journey with you in this life is over. They were meant to be there for a season, and for a certain reason, and they fulfilled that reason. All you have to do is be graceful, move with grace at all times.

In the end, remember that life is short, and that we are here to please Allah and not others, enjoy your company, and surround yourself with people you respect, and love. Surround yourself with high vibrational people. If you lose

someone you were really close with, it just means Allah is
making room for great people to come into your life, it is
time for you to elevate. Remember you are a king/queen –
carry yourself that way :)

Advise about the Hijab

Did you know that Allah's Hijab is light? The most High is
also hidden from this world, and will only reveal himself on
the first Friday in Paradise. This hijab that you wear is a
commandment of Allah but there is so much wisdom behind
it, cherish it and love it. Remember that Mary the mother of
Jesus, also covered from head to toe and all the greatest
women to walk this earth – who will all be the VIPs of
paradise one day.

Remember that hijab represents that you are demanding
respect, that you are defined by your personality,
characteristics, and essence as a human and not your looks,
body, and beauty.

For those who are thinking of wearing it, intention matters, don't wear it for others or due to societal pressures, if it is not for Allah – then that wouldn't define worship. Take your time to understand it and slowly work your way towards it if you have to. Remember this is your choice, and not anyone else to decide. Remember that the stories in the Quran contain gems of wisdom that we can apply to our lives and I hope that the content in this book provides you with valuable insight on the Quran and Islamic sciences.

In conclusion, this is the 2nd series to an ongoing series, insha'Allah the next book will be out soon and when it is look-out for an announcement on my Instagram page. I appreciate all of you, for your continued support and encouragement. I wish all of you the best of luck in all of your future endeavors, and that you achieve all of your dreams and goals in life.

Your sister,
Amal Maow

Made in United States
North Haven, CT
07 August 2022

22359032R10176